Understanding Physic
Development in the F

Understanding Physical Development in the Early Years provides an accessible introduction to the current research and thinking in this area alongside descriptions of everyday practice. It explores the kinds of activities and experiences that promote physical development and offers practical guidance on how these can be facilitated.

Physical development plays a crucial role in young children's learning, behaviour and emotional health and is recognised as a Prime area in the revised Early Years Foundation Stage. It is therefore essential that those working in the early years sector provide children with a wide range of opportunities for movement and sensory experiences.

Drawing on current legislation and the requirements of the EYFS, the book covers all aspects of physical development and includes:

- reflection tasks, summaries and impact on practice sections;

- guidance on issues that can cause concern such as health and safety, rough and tumble play, gender and the effective use of indoor and outdoor space;

- advice on the role of the practitioner and ideas for working with parents and families;

- information on the different stages of physical development.

Written by leading consultants, this book will be essential reading for early years students and practitioners who want to fully understand young children's physical development and provide opportunities that nourish children's overall learning and physical and emotional wellbeing.

Anne O'Connor is an experienced teacher, with specialist knowledge in the Early Years Foundation Stage, currently working as an independent consultant, trainer and writer.

Anna Daly is an experienced independent community dance artist, trainer and lecturer, with specialist knowledge in early years and family work.

Understanding Physical Development in the Early Years

Linking bodies and minds

Anne O'Connor and Anna Daly

Routledge
Taylor & Francis Group

LONDON AND NEW YORK

First published 2016
by Routledge
2 Park Square, Milton Park, Abingdon, Oxon OX14 4RN

and by Routledge
711 Third Avenue, New York, NY 10017

Routledge is an imprint of the Taylor & Francis Group, an informa business

British Library Cataloguing in Publication Data
A catalogue record for this book is available from the British Library

Library of Congress Cataloging in Publication Data
Names: Daly, Anna, author. | O'Connor, Anne, 1957- author.
Title: Understanding physical development in the early years : linking
bodies and minds / Anna Daly and Anne O'Connor.
Description: Abingdon, Oxon ; New York, NY : Routledge, [2016]
Identifiers: LCCN 2015037385 | ISBN 9780415722476 (hbk) | ISBN
9780415722483 (pbk) | ISBN 9781315640136 (ebk)
Subjects: LCSH: Physical education for children. | Early childhood
education.
Classification: LCC GV443 .D27 2016 | DDC 372.86--dc23
LC record available at http://lccn.loc.gov/2015037385

ISBN: 978-0-415-72247-6 (hbk)
ISBN: 978-0-415-72248-3 (pbk)
ISBN: 978-1-315-64013-6 (ebk)

Typeset in Melior
by Saxon Graphics Ltd, Derby

Printed and bound by CPI Group (UK) Ltd, Croydon, CR0 4YY

AO'C For Carlene Hutchinson-Norris and Denise Bailey: colleagues and friends for life.

AD For all the atypical children, whose stories we can hear if only we 'tune in'.

Contents

Acknowledgements

We would like to thank all the practitioners, children and their families with whom we have worked who have stimulated our interest in this subject and helped increase our knowledge and understanding. We would particularly like to thank Jenny Davies of Ryelands Primary School and Yvette Pullen of Ridge Primary School, both in Lancaster, for their contributions.

Thanks also to Anna Vardos and Zsuzsa Libertiny of the Pikler Institute in Budapest, Dr Lala Manners of Active Matters and Gill Connell of Moving Smart, who generously gave of their time to answer questions and provide information – and particularly to Lala and Gill for their continued support!

A big thank you to Orla, for tolerating us as we observed her physical development over the first two years of her life, photographing her every move. Thank you to her brother, Jem, for his contribution and we are very grateful to their parents Tanya and Jed Williamson for permission to use their photographs. Thanks also to Jake and Shanice Norris for their photograph of Ariana.

We would also like to thank Ruth Thomson and Liz Roberts of *Nursery World*, who initiated the original request for the series of articles that first brought us together in a professional capacity and triggered the creation of 'Primed for Life Training Associates'.

We are very grateful to all the writers, educators, therapists and movement and dance specialists whose ideas and thinking have inspired us to write this book.

Anna would like to thank: my parents for fostering my early love of movement, music and dance. My Mr D. Thank you and much love, always. To Anne, my friend, colleague and collaborator, thank you for the incredible stories you share from your experience and lifelong commitment to early education. You inspire me to keep asking questions on behalf of the children. Thanks for being a partner in curiosity and learning – long may we continue to discover what we do not yet know.

Anne wishes to say a big THANK YOU to all the family and friends who have continued to provide support and encouragement during the lengthy writing process. You know who you are. Particular thanks go to Wendy Scott for her constancy and her practical support in providing a peaceful refuge for writing whenever it was needed. To Anna Daly must go huge thanks and appreciation for being prepared to collaborate with me and for bringing such a wealth of knowledge and perspectives from the world of dance. Much respect. To my son, Danny, thanks and love always.

Thank you to everyone at Taylor and Francis involved in the editing and production of this book.

Introduction

I believe that the unity of mind and body is an objective reality. They are not just parts somehow related to each other, but an inseparable whole while functioning. A brain without a body could not think... the muscles themselves are part and parcel of our higher functions.

(Feldenkrais 1980)

Primed for Life Training Associates came into being when an early years consultant and a community dance artist came together to write a series on physical development for *Nursery World*, a UK national early years magazine. We found that our individual perspectives, coming from the worlds of education and dance, met in a mutual concern to improve the quality of experience for young children, by raising the status of physical development among both practitioners and parents. We were both fascinated by the link between movement and brain development and struck by the clear indications that primitive reflexes had a large (but often unrecognised) role to play in children's learning development and in their emotional as well as physical wellbeing.

However, the designation of physical development as a Prime area in the revisions to the Foundation Stage in 2012 brought PD into the forefront of the early years curriculum – and gave us a name for the training work we do together. Yet 'Primed for Life' is more than just a catchy name and slogan. It sums up how we feel about this important aspect of early child development. Along with the two other Prime areas, Communication and Language (CL) and Personal, Social and Emotional Development (PSED), Physical Development (PD) is fundamental, not just for learning, but for the adventure of life itself.

We continue to have concerns about many aspects of the current EYFS framework, but with this development has come a gradual shift in understanding of the nature of the Specific areas, and in particular literacy and numeracy, in relation to early child development. It is now more formally recognised (in format, if not always in practice) that these areas are reliant on an essential foundation of other developmental processes and experience, without which they will only progress (if at all) in superficial and unsupported ways.

As an example, the majority of us have learnt how to handwrite with a pen – a fundamental aspect of literacy. Not all of us have legible handwriting, however, or can handwrite for any length of time without our muscles becoming tired and achy and the quality of our writing deteriorating. Despite what we might have been led to believe in school, this is not due to lack of effort on our part, or some innate failing that meant the harder we tried, the worse our handwriting became. It is much more likely to be a result of being made to engage in a fine motor skill too early. Young children will always explore mark making, especially if there is something messy to make marks with. But at the same time, our bodies need to engage in a sufficient amount of gross motor experience in order for our fine motor skills to even begin to develop fully. This experience will ultimately enable our brain and body to communicate well enough to hold the pencil in the optimum way to form the letters neatly, with enough pressure to make suitable marks, but without so much pressure that our fingers and wrists soon become tired, and our marks are so heavy they print through several pages! However, there will be some of us for whom, even though we might have learnt the mechanics of writing, know how the letters are formed and may even be skilful and imaginative with words, our ability to perform the task with 'mastery' is always going to be limited. For those of us for whom this is the case, there will no doubt be very unhappy memories of enforced practice to improve, and a sense of injustice that no matter how hard we tried, our work would always be judged harshly because of our poor handwriting. How different our lives might have been if our parents and teachers had been advised by the likes of Gill Connell, co-author of *A Moving Child is a Learning Child: How the Body Teaches the Brain to Think* (2014), who tells concerned parents and teachers that the best way to improve their children's handwriting skills is to 'Put your pencils down and go play on the monkey bars' (Connell and McCarthy 2014:135).

This is because there is a natural order to body control and the larger muscles need to be well developed before they can support the complexities of the many smaller muscles, bones, ligaments and tendons of the hands. There are also primitive hand reflexes that have powerful reasons for their existence in the earliest months of a child's life, but are detrimental to the use and control of the hands if they are still there at a later age. Those reflexes need to be 'inhibited' – and playing on the monkey bars is an excellent way to do this, as are all the different kinds of movement play that we expect to see in young children.

But our educational practices often interfere with that natural order, by placing too much emphasis on fine motor control, much too soon, before the physical developmental process is ready and the hands are 'primed' for writing.

As the educational climate becomes even more pressurised with an emphasis on formal aspects of academic learning at an increasingly young age, this is an important enough reason by itself for us to want to promote a greater understanding of physical development. But not only must the Prime areas be in place in order for the Specific areas to be able to develop well, they also 'prime' our bodies and brains for the very act of life itself, so that we can live well, in addition to being able to learn well.

Early years specialists, and those in the field of motor and sensory development, have long believed that the generation of the nervous system and the development of the brain depended on early movement and sensory experience. We now have the neuroscientific technology to be able to confirm some of those suppositions and theories. This includes a greater understanding of the links between the vestibular and proprioceptive systems and our emotional health and wellbeing (e.g. Mast et al. 2014). However, as always, there is the danger that when new technology leads us to a little bit of increased knowledge, it results in a whole new 'bandwagon' of practice for everyone to jump on and 'the promulgation of a range of neuromyths and misdiagnoses resulting from oversimplifications and overgeneralisations of early research and often tentative findings' (Whitebread and Sinclair-Harding 2014). But even neuroscientists seem to agree that the more we find out about the brain, the less we know for certain (Nurse 2009:18).

What is clear, however, is

* Children's brains are changed by experience. Good experiences are required for good brain development and expression of genetic potential. Most of the brain's development after birth is dependent on experience, which needs to be repetitive, consistent and in a context of emotional and social security.*

(Winter 2010)

This statement comes from a document produced by the Australian Ministerial Council for Education, Early Childhood Development and Youth Affairs outlining significant neuroscientific research and the implications for practice with families of young children. They too caution against the overuse of neuroscience in defining practice but conclude that there is significant evidence to suggest that, although negative early experiences are not irredeemable, the first five years really do matter – and the impact of those first five years can last a lifetime.

That is why we do not offer in this book, or in our training, a 'programme' of activities to accelerate physical development or an exercise 'package' to promote health and early skills attainment. This book is not about 'accelerating' learning or 'hot housing' physical skills. Rather, what we hope to encourage, in our writing and training work, is support for the provision of environments that nurture the kind of natural, instinctive physical progression with which, unfortunately, modern day life often interferes. These environments will allow us to fill in some of the 'gaps' that, for one reason or another, any of our children might experience in their earliest years. To do this it is necessary to bring together two very important elements of early years practice – observation (as a means of really getting to know an individual child well and being able to 'attune' to their developmental needs) matched with a sound knowledge of child development. Our experience, however, has been that practitioners at all levels of qualification rarely receive detailed tuition or information about early physical development and that curriculum guidance generally contains sparse information on the subject, beyond hygiene and healthy eating advice. Our aim therefore, is to provide accessible explanations of the 'science' of physical development alongside meaningful examples of how early physical experiences can affect our quality of life and learning, both as children and as adults.

Organisation of chapters

Many of the different aspects of physical development are interlinked – this means that some aspects will be revisited with a different emphasis depending on the context of individual chapters.

Chapter 1 provides background information about what we mean by physical development in relation to early childhood care and education. As well as considering why it is so important, we also look at the links between movement and the brain. Despite this crucial relationship, we must also consider why physical development has been ignored and underrated over the years, in comparison with other areas of development. Chapter 2 focuses on our own attitudes as adults and the early experiences that have helped form those beliefs and dispositions. Relating to those experiences encourages us to connect with our individual physicality and helps us 'step into the shoes of the child', which in turn informs our practice. In Chapter 3 we explore the stages of physical development, looking at the processes involved in locomotion and the importance of children moving through these stages at their own pace.

Linked to this is the integration of primitive reflexes, which we look at in depth in Chapter 4, considering why they exist and the problems related to their continued existence, long after they are needed. Chapters 5 and 6 consider the importance of good sensory processing and the impact of the vestibular and proprioceptive senses in particular. Finally, Chapter 7 considers the role of physical development in the early years curriculum and the ways that dance and movement play support all areas of learning. Chapters 3–7 also contain a section devoted to 'Playful Ideas' to take some of the theory off the page and into practice. Although some ideas may seem age-specific, they can also be adapted to suit children at most stages of development within the EYFS and even beyond. Use them spontaneously, responding 'in the moment' to what your observations tell you about a child's developmental readiness, as well as in short bursts of structured activity in small groups, if and when appropriate.

Each chapter contains reflection tasks that also link theory with practice and allow the reader to reflect personally on their own experiences as well as their opinions, judgements and motivations. Sections relating to partnerships with parents and other professionals conclude each chapter, together with a chapter summary and implications for practice. Further ideas for resources, equipment and more information are also included at the end of the book. We endeavour to explain complicated or unfamiliar terms as we introduce them, but a glossary is also included, for further reference.

A note on terminology

There continues to be debate about the best ways of labelling the various roles within the early years workforce. We have chosen to continue with the practice of referring to everyone who is qualified to work with babies and young children as early years 'practitioners'. This includes those with teaching qualifications, education and early childhood degrees, as well as Early Years Professionals (EYP), Nursery Nurses (NNEB), those with NVQ qualifications and the recently introduced Early Years Teacher Status (EYTS). They may be working in childminding, in childcare and nursery settings, in schools or play worker organisations. This book also serves as a resource for community dance artists and those working in dance in education – a field in which the term practitioner is also in regular use. As 'practitioners', we all share a common goal in the quality of our practice with young children and their families, and the care with which we attend to their developmental needs.

What is physical development and why is it so important?

This chapter reflects on our understanding of physical development, considers why increased knowledge and understanding of this Prime area of the EYFS is so important and introduces some of the key issues.

What do we mean by physical development?

> **HAVE A THINK ABOUT...** THE WORDS YOU ASSOCIATE WITH THE TERM 'PHYSICAL DEVELOPMENT'
>
> Here are a few that usually come up when we ask people this question:
>
> - Bodies. Muscles. Limbs. Health. Growth. Running. Sport. PE. Heart and lungs. Babies and toddlers. Health checks. Maturation. Milestones. Gross motor skills. Fine motor skills. Locomotion. Movement. Hygiene. Using tools.
>
> What kind of information about physical development did you have in your initial training? How important do you think it is in your work?

> I've always been more interested in language and early literacy; I thought physical development was just about PE and stuff – but now I know what it is really all about I can't wait to get back to my setting and do things differently!

This is the kind of comment we hear all the time from people who attend our courses on physical development. So much so that we would like to give this area a completely different name! As you will see throughout this book, physical development (PD) is clearly about the development of movement and all the relevant stages contributing to locomotion, but it also includes the development of the brain, which is inextricably linked with the development of the body and vice versa! *Neurophysiological* development is a term used by some specialists, to describe the interdependent nature of body and brain development, which also includes the integration of the senses and the development of a fully functioning nervous system, leading to the growth of a happy and healthy individual.

A child's physical development includes:

- Growth and control of limbs, muscles, joints, bladder, bowel etc.

- Motor development leading to bipedal (upright on two legs) mobility

- Inhibition of primitive reflexes

- Sensory development including vestibular and proprioceptive senses

- Fine and gross motor skills

- Mastery of a range of physical skills, locomotion, dynamic balance, agility, physical literacy, manipulating tools etc.

The most common understanding of physical development is probably physical growth. It seems an obvious place to begin, because growth can be an indicator of healthy development even before birth.

Measuring growth

The measurement of children's physical growth and development begins in the womb, with measurements being taken and the mother's weight gain identifying the health of the pregnancy. After the announcement of the birth and enquiry about a new baby's gender (if not already known) and general health, then the next piece of information offered is always about weight and sometimes length. We associate weights within a certain margin with healthiness, and babies are monitored to ensure steady weight gain. Height (length) too is regularly checked along with head size in the first year. We judge whether or not these measurements are increasing within typical margins by referring to centile charts. These plot the head circumference, weight and length of babies in order to compare the pattern of growth of an individual child against a larger number of children of the same age and gender. Centile charts can provide reassurance that, within a certain range, a child is developing at a 'typical' rate. Figures outside of this range would suggest that a child's development is less typical and possibly requires monitoring. Using the word 'typical' is more useful here than 'normal', which has lots of value judgement attached to it and isn't strictly accurate if we accept that babies are born unique and develop in uniquely individual ways! We will look more closely at the concept of 'typical' and 'atypical' development later in this chapter.

Look how you've grown!

It is easy, then, to focus on the external, very visible growth of a child from babyhood. Measurements are recorded regularly and parents and health professionals are reassured by a child's steady growth. We emphasise growth as a sign of maturation and as adults we compliment children on how big they have grown (Maude 2001), and, rather ridiculously, we express surprise that they have grown when we haven't seen them for a while! For some of us, adult interest in our growth as children (too much or not enough) might have been a cause of anxiety or even distress, much of which the adults might have been unaware.

HAVE A THINK ABOUT... YOUR OWN EXPERIENCES OF PHYSICALLY GROWING

What do you remember from your own childhood as a marker of your growth?

Your clothes? Wearing clothes that were too small or too short as you grew fast? Wearing clothes that were too big or too long so you could 'grow into them'?

Did you have a regular marker on the wall or a doorpost?

Do you remember wanting to be tall enough to reach or see over something?

For one of the authors it was being able to see over the tall counter in the chip shop, for the other, finally being tall enough to go on the big rides at the fairground.

Were you aware of adult interest in your growth – height or weight?

How did this make you feel?

Has it made a difference to the way you comment on children's growth?

Concerns about obesity

With the current focus on childhood obesity, even more attention is being paid to young children's size and weight than ever before. Concerns about the quality and quantity of a child's diet and nutritional intake and the focus on 'healthy eating' in the current Early Learning Goals (ELGs) in England, place a shared responsibility on carers as well as parents to monitor children's nutritional intake.

We must be careful that this emphasis on the external evidence of physical growth and maturation doesn't overshadow the growth and development taking place internally, as children's sensory and nervous systems develop. This kind of development is harder to measure, which perhaps explains why it features less in the public awareness – and also in any statutory requirements. But as many specialists in the subject have suggested, the less obvious physical developments of early childhood have an equal, if not more powerful, impact on future health, emotional wellbeing and learning potential (Goddard Blythe 2004, 2009; Ayres 1972, 2005; Hannaford 2005; Maude 2001; Nurse 2009).

From top to bottom and side to side

Two processes, both with rather complicated names, determine motor development, although the processes themselves are quite straightforward to understand.

Cephalocaudal development refers to development that is 'top-down'. 'Cephalo' stems from the Greek word 'kephale' which means 'head'. Other words that are similar are encephalitis (inflammation of the brain) and hydrocephalus (fluid build up in the skull affecting the brain). 'Cauda' stems from the Latin word for 'tail' so cephalocaudal refers to motor and muscular development that spreads from 'head to tail' or in the case of humans 'from head to toe'. Patricia Maude (2001:8) suggests this makes a lot of sense if you consider that in a human newborn it is the head that is most well developed, in order to house the brain that is already controlling all bodily functions, whilst the legs and feet are still relatively undeveloped and not yet able to provide mobility. Maude explains that

> Muscular development follows the same top-down sequence: control of the head is achieved prior to musculature to gain control of the shoulders. Once the infant can hold up the head unaided, the spinal muscles develop to enable the sitting position to be achieved, aided and then unaided.
>
> (2001:8)

The legs begin to gain strength only when creeping and crawling begin and they are needed to help propel the body along. As the legs grow in strength, they become able to bear weight and eventually are strong enough for standing and walking, growing stronger throughout childhood and into adulthood. This top-down growth and development continues as the musculature supporting the feet and ankles matures and strengthens, enabling increased efficiency in movement and propulsion (Maude 2001:8).

Proximo-distal development describes the process of movement control emerging and extending from the 'proximal' (close to the body) out to the 'distal' (furthest from the centre of the body). So, just like the cephalocaudal process, the first part of the word describes where the control is most developed at birth. The 'proximal' space is nearer to the centre of the body, but the functions of the 'distal' parts of the body (the arms, hands and fingers) are underdeveloped at first, as they are not needed for things like pushing and pulling or manipulating until later. So as Maude describes, 'the musculature to the shoulder girdle gains strength before that to the elbows, wrists, hands and finally to the fingers'(Maude 2001:8). Because of this, we see small babies at first only able to swing their whole arm to swipe or 'bat' at a hanging mobile. Later, the shoulder muscles will allow them to bring both arms to the centre to 'clap hands' or take something in a two-handed grasp well before they have the coordination and muscle strength to use their hands for different purposes at the same time. It can be several years before there is enough differentiation in the joints and muscles of the wrists and hands to enable the fingers to be used efficiently. This has implications for our expectations of the age at which children should begin formal handwriting. Children are often interested in mark making at an early age. They enjoy drawing, painting and mimicking adults writing for a purpose, e.g. signing their name, making lists etc. But this scientific information does suggest that we need to allow adequate time for the proximo-distal process to fully develop at its own pace and not rush immature joints and muscles into positions and activities for which they are not yet ready.

> If children are required to form legible letters and are given writing tasks before the developmental processes of bone differentiation and strengthening of the muscles to the wrist bones have adequately been achieved, the result can be frustration and inhibition in achievement.
>
> (Maude 2001:10–11)

In the UK, children are often expected to begin practising their handwriting at age four and often younger. And yet there are lots of concerns about the quality of handwriting in older children and the range of inappropriate pencil holds. As a contrast, in France, although children play with crayons, pencils and paints from an early age, they don't begin formal handwriting until they are of compulsory school age between six and seven years old, when they learn cursive writing from the start.

HAVE A THINK ABOUT... HANDWRITING AS A FINE MOTOR SKILL

Are you a good hand writer, or were you always berated for untidy or illegible writing? Do you remember struggling to stay on the line, or to form letters neatly in a row?

At what age do you think children should begin formal handwriting as opposed to free mark making? How do you think this affects their emerging compositional and imaginative skills?

What role do you think handwriting will play in the future as children develop keyboard and touch screen skills at an earlier age?

What difference do you think current and future technology, e.g. phone and computer keyboards, touch screens etc. will make to the development of fine motor skills?

Why is physical development so important?

Physical health

Obviously physical development is linked with children's health and their ability to thrive and flourish. The pioneers of nursery education in the last century were very clear about the benefits of movement and physical activity, particularly for underprivileged children, and that need is still very valid in these times of economic austerity. But the economic status of their parents does not always protect children from the impact of limited movement and physical activity in their earliest years. We will look more closely in later chapters at the significant changes in child rearing that have had an impact on children's early movement experiences, but one of the key issues is the lengthy periods children can spend strapped into car seats and pushchairs that inhibit natural movements. Another is the heightened fears that many parents express about risky play and unsupervised play outdoors, leading to a generation (and more) of children whose physical play experiences are limited, regardless of their parents' economic wellbeing. We will discover, as we look more closely at different aspects of physical development in the early years, that there is a wide range of health issues linked to children's lack of physical activity. As well as obvious concerns about obesity and related medical conditions (e.g. diabetes) these also include postural disorders (e.g. torticollis – distortion of the neck due to restricted movement) and difficulties with toilet training, visual perception and sensory processing.

Impact on children's wellbeing

Physical development has a fundamental role to play in all of the other areas of learning, and we will consider these in greater depth in Chapter 7 when we look at physical development within the EYFS. Sally Goddard Blythe reminds us of the intrinsic way in which PD is linked with emotional wellbeing, by calling her book *The Well Balanced Child*, highlighting the connections between physical balance and emotional equilibrium – a state of mental composure and stability.

Movement Play Specialists, Jabadao, engaged in a ten-year study in early years settings that highlighted the links between movement play and children's wellbeing. As a result of their investigations, they put together a programme of 'Developmental Movement Play' (DMP). This combines developmental movement theory with a play-based, child-led movement approach that draws on their specialism as dancers and that has had a positive impact on both the children and practitioners involved, particularly with regard to wellbeing. Using the Leuven scales of Wellbeing and Involvement (Laevers 1994), their research showed children had increased levels of wellbeing in all the following areas when they were engaged in movement play:

- Enjoyment
- Relaxing and inner peace
- Vitality
- Openness
- Self confidence
- Being in touch with oneself.

(Jabadao 2009)

We will explore emotional wellbeing in greater depth in later chapters.

Impact on children's learning

The Jabadao research highlighted the difficulties that exist for practitioners who have had inadequate training and guidance to support PD. This support is needed more than ever if we take into account the results of a study measuring the physical development and neuromotor skills of Foundation Stage children against their 'readiness' for school. This was the first study of its kind and it found that children who struggled to sit still or hold a pencil might not have fully completed steps in their neurophysiological development as babies (Griffin 2011, cited in Morton 2012).

This is confirmed by Sally Goddard Blythe's comment that 'there are children who are five year olds on the outside but three year olds in terms of their motor skills' (Goddard Blythe, cited in Gaunt 2011).

The suggestion here is that the internal processes required to build the sensory and neuromotor skills needed for the kinds of activities associated (not always appropriately) with entry into school are lacking in some children. These include sitting still and writing with a pencil. This is considered to be a result of limited physical experiences, such as floor play and crawling, which support both the physical and the neurological development required for such activities. It is as if, long before children can acquire the skills we associate with literacy, they must first acquire '*physical literacy*' skills – a breadth of sensory and movement abilities and experiences that will support the specifics of later life in school. Some of these are obvious. It is easy to see how we need fine motor control of the hands and fingers to use a pencil – but, as already noted, it's perhaps not so obvious that we need a whole range of gross motor experiences, involving the head, neck, shoulder and arm, before we are ever going to be ready to use our fingers to hold and manipulate a pencil in a grip suitable for neat handwriting. Without this knowledge, it is likely that a range of inappropriate remedial activities may be suggested for a child who appears to be 'failing' rather than them being provided with the opportunity to revisit and explore earlier essential gross motor activities that they have missed out on.

HAVE A THINK ABOUT... THE CONCEPT OF 'SCHOOL READINESS'

What do you think children need in order to be 'ready for school'?

How do you know when a child is 'school ready'?

How do you assess a child's 'physical' readiness for school?

What skills and abilities would you consider to be essential for 'physical literacy'?

You might like to ask yourself these questions again when you reach the end of the book.

Brain development

Neuroscientific research is constantly updating our knowledge about the way the brain works though we are still a long way from knowing everything.

'The brain has been described as the last unexplored territory on earth, but many neuroscientists would say that the more we find out, the less we seem to know for certain' (Nurse 2009:18).

Shaping the brain

So what does neuroscience currently have to tell us about the way a baby's brain is shaped and developed?

- Babies are born with more brain cells (neurons) than they are going to need.

- However, they need to make connections (synapses) between these neurons in order to build and develop the architecture of the brain.

- Those connections are made through experience of different stimuli—sensations of touch, taste, smell, sight, hearing, vestibular signals, proprioception and movement.

- The more repetitions of those experiences, the stronger the connections, and the 'clearer' the pathways from one part of the body (or brain) to another.

- This is helped by a process called 'myelination' that insulates the nerves, helping to create strong neural pathways and some 'super highways' that lead to speedy reactions.

- This also leaves the higher part of the brain free to deal with the tricky stuff of rational thought and coping with emotions.

- Connections that don't become strong through repetition get 'pruned away' – it's as if the brain prioritises what is most useful (i.e. being used the most) and doesn't hang on to the rest.

- It is perfectly possible to create new connections at a later stage but it takes more effort.

- Some connections are time-sensitive and happen more easily at certain times.

- Some connections can't be made if the body and the brain aren't ready for them – they rely on other connections being made first.

- Pushing 'practice' when the brain/body are not sufficiently mature and ready may do actual harm as inappropriate neural pathways may develop, affecting longer-term development as well as motivation.

(Adapted from Nurse 2009 and Pound 2013)

The nervous system

The nervous system runs throughout the body. It is made up of the brain, the spinal cord and peripheral nerves. The brain is the 'head quarters' of the nervous system (Biswas-Diener 2015).

What do we need to know about the nervous system?

■ Neurologists consider the nervous system to be in two parts.

● The **central nervous system** (CNS) consists of the brain and the spinal cord.

● The **peripheral nervous system** (PNS) is made up of all the nerve fibres branching off from the spinal cord and extending to all parts of the body including the neck and limbs, torso, muscles and internal organs.

■ Messages are carried throughout the nervous system by **neurons** which consist of a nucleus and its extensions (**axons** and **dendrites**).

■ These make connections with the axons and dendrites of other neurons, which is how they communicate with each other.

■ When one neuron receives a message from another, it sends an electrical signal down to the end of its axon where it is converted into a chemical signal.

■ The axon releases **neurotransmitters** (chemical messengers) into the space between the end of the axon and the tip of the dendrite belonging to the other neuron.

■ The space between the two is called a synapse and the receiving dendrite converts the neurotransmitters back into an electrical signal that travels through the neuron.

■ This is then converted back into a chemical signal when it reaches other neurons.

■ **Motor neurons** control voluntary movement by transmitting messages in the form of electrical impulses FROM the brain or spinal cord to the muscles.

■ **Sensory neurons** send information TO the brain from incoming messages from the senses.

■ Involuntary processes involved in organ and glandular function such as digestive regulation and the release of hormones are also regulated by the nervous system.

■ Communicating neurons connect up to form lots of neural networks in the brain, capable of working together and enabling different parts of the brain to connect with each other.

(Adapted from Society for Neuroscience 2015
and NICHD 2014)

Nerve networks

These neural networks of thoughts and reactions become increasingly complex as more and more pathways are created carrying electrochemical impulses around the body. And as Carla Hannaford points out, 'these ever branching pathways are in a continual state of becoming. As long as the stimulation continues, more dendritic branching occurs. If the stimuli stop, the branching stops. These pathways alter from moment to moment throughout our lives' (Hannaford 2005:28, citing Diamond 1988).

This is good news as it reminds us that learning is a lifelong matter and that we can create new pathways in our brains no matter how old we get. See Chapter 2 for more on neural pathways.

Movement and the brain

Crucial to the formation of neural networks is physical movement or *'physical action'*, which, Linda Pound suggests, is 'much more than health; much more than independence, much more than wellbeing. It is the means by which we survive' (Pound 2013:5).

Carol Archer and Iram Siraj in their book *Encouraging Physical Development through Movement Play* (2015) are equally emphatic on the importance of movement to nerve cell growth. 'Movement stimulates the neurological system that fires and wires the brain, forming a multitude of connections that lay important foundations for the young child's future learning and development' (Archer and Siraj 2015:1)

Our biological drive to move

Linda Pound also quotes Susan Greenfield's suggestion that 'if we didn't move we wouldn't need a brain' (Greenfield 1996:34, cited in Pound 2013:5) This is such a powerful statement as it draws our attention to the way that the development of the brain is intrinsically linked to movement.

If we need a brain because we move, then movement must be important to the brain. It's another chicken and egg situation. Do we have a brain because we move? Can we only move because we've got a brain? Either way, we have to concede that movement and the brain are linked in ways that many of us may simply never have thought about, beyond assuming that the brain controls our movements. A better understanding of physical development in general, and neurophysiological development in particular, allows us to see just how important spontaneous movement play is in developing the architecture of our brains – and why limited physical experiences in the early years can have major implications for children's all round development.

Movement and thinking

Carla Hannaford, author of *Smart Moves: Why Learning Is Not All in Your Head* comments that 'Movement anchors thought' (Hannaford 2005:109). She describes how often we find that we need a physical movement to help us remember or clarify a thought. Are you one of those people who like to write lists? Do you sometimes find that once you have written the list you don't often refer back to it? For some of us, the physical act of writing, which has involved movement in the hands, wrist, arm and positioning of the body, 'anchors' our thought process and helps us not just to remember things, but to problem solve and clarify ideas so that our thoughts are useful to us. Talking also helps us with our thought processes and involves lots of facial movements – and sometimes lots of hand waving and gesturing as many of us 'talk with our hands' and not just our mouths. When learning new information it is often very helpful to talk about it soon afterwards, to help clarify and embed the new knowledge. The best teachers know this and provide opportunities for learners (of any age) to talk about their learning as a fundamental part of the process.

Similarly, many of us find that we think better when involved in low-concentration, repetitive, physical activity. For some of us that might be swimming, running or just going for a walk. For others it might be a household task like ironing or gardening, or even just tapping or fiddling with something in our hands, like a pen or piece of string. For a young child, thought and movement will be even more closely linked as their ability to rationalise thought *before* acting will be very limited. Something attracts their attention (triggering their thinking process) and they are likely to move towards it, reaching out to bring it into their grasp. A sad thought will trigger instant facial expression, accompanied by verbal expression (a cry or wail) and probably tears, all of which involve face muscles and possibly the shaking of arms, clenching of fists and stamping of feet. And the same is true of happy feelings, expressed not just through smiles, but also through sounds and excited body movements. Movement helps young children to think, just as it does for adults, and yet we tend to assume fidgeting and fiddling with things to be evidence of poor concentration and a lack of attention. But if you have ever doodled your way through a lesson or lecture – or even a phone call – you will be aware of just how much it can help your concentration.

Movement as communication

Movement *is* our first form of communication. Think of how a foetus in the womb makes itself known – by kicking and moving around. It's also how the foetus responds to stimulus from within the mother or from outside; most pregnant women report that extra kicks and movements can occur in response to the mother's choice of lunch or as a result of loud noises or things that startle the mother.

Non-verbal communication continues to be important, even from the moment a baby is born, when the caring touch and hold of another human being communicates the most important thing a baby needs to know in those first few moments. 'No words are necessary for a newborn to understand what love feels like' (Connell and McCarthy 2014:145), and a parent who is able to tune in instinctively to the wriggles, fidgets, kicks and waves of their small baby knows that movement always accompanies sound whether the baby is crying with frustration or cooing with delight. Whatever their baby is trying to express through vocalisation, the child's legs and arms will probably be in motion as well as their head and mouth muscles. In the days before sophisticated methods of measuring brain waves, researchers would refer to a baby's kicking as a way of measuring response to a familiar stimulus and Goddard Blythe suggests that wriggling of the toes and feet will often occur just before a baby is about to babble (Goddard Blythe 2009). Watch out for this if you happen to have a baby nearby to observe!

Body language and non-verbal communication

This is such an important feature of early communication and language development, and one that is intrinsically linked with a child's physical development and their movement ability. Children learn a lot through mimicry and imitation, and before they have complete comprehension of the words and vocabulary, they gain more through how we say something than what we actually say. As their vocabulary and understanding grow, it is the combination of verbal and non-verbal communication together that increases the quality of the interaction and aids learning. Not only does 'physical language' (Connell and McCarthy 2014:145), such as facial expression, posture and gesture and the exaggerated mouth movements and sing-song tone of voice we instinctively use with very young children, increase the likelihood of understanding, it also creates a multi-sensory experience for the child which can trigger 'intellectual and emotional connections in the brain that leave lasting impressions and provide a model he can use to express himself someday' (Connell and McCarthy 2014:145).

Movement as expression

As Carla Hannaford describes, 'Movement gives our faces the ability to express joy, sadness, anger and love in our very human quest to be understood' (Hannaford 2005:108). It also enables us to show our emotions in our stance and in our gestures. Young children seem to absorb this information very quickly. A toddler expressing her desire not to leave the park may well stand with her legs planted firmly and her arms folded across her chest, already aware of the body language that expresses resistance and intent, or she may equally roll around on the floor kicking and screaming!

But movement also enables us to express our response to stimuli, particularly music, either in choreographed moves or improvised, dancing to the radio in the kitchen or in a nightclub. Movement of the mouth and lips is key to singing or whistling. Making instrumental music involves movement of the arms and hands usually (at the very least), although often the whole body is in motion, as it also often is when singing. Art involves movement of the hands and arms (and sometimes other body parts) as well as the head and neck and eye muscles. Theatre and drama are rarely still and often involve exaggerated movements, particularly in mime, to express meaning. Even if we are not involved in the creation of art, music or drama, our main response to it as an audience is very often in the vigorous movement of bringing our hands together and clapping – or, if we are deaf, in waving both hands at the players.

Cultural body language

It is worth remembering that although non-verbal communication is universal across the world, the actual content of it can vary enormously. A posture or stance (e.g. not making eye contact) that in one culture signals deference or courtesy may in another be judged as insolent, rude or impolite. In some countries a shake of the head means no, whereas in others (Bangladesh, for example) a quick head tilt to the side signifies a qualified acceptance ('yes, maybe'). Getting to really know the communities and cultural languages of the children and families we work with can make a big difference to our understanding of their body language and non-verbal communication and improve the quality of our interactions.

Movement as self-actualisation

Carla Hannaford describes how movement in the womb gives us our first sense of gravity and the beginnings of our understanding of the world. 'The rhythmic movements of our mother's walking, before and after birth, her rocking, breathing, heart rhythms, all set up coherent patterns that assist us to understand the patterns within math, language, and natural science' (Hannaford 2005:107).

For the very young child, gaining mobility enables independence and the ability to put 'will into action'. A baby who can crawl is able to follow its mother around, rather than having to rely on their cries to keep her close. If they see something enticing across the room, they can set off and go check it out for themselves. They are also engaging in constant physical problem solving. 'How do I get down off this chair?' 'What happens if I crawl backwards?' 'Can I run down the slope without falling over?'

Learning how to work with gravity is fundamental to our early movement experiencing, and achieving 'gravitational security' is a key element in our physical development. Ray Barsch reminds us of this fact by referring to babies as 'terranauts' learning to negotiate gravity on the 'terra firma' of planet earth, just as astronauts have to learn to handle the lack of gravity out in space (Barsch 1968, cited in Goddard Blythe 2004:175).

Importance of movement play

'Movement-play is about children moving in specific ways as they go through a developmental sequence of significant movement patterns that link the body and the brain' (Archer and Siraj 2015:1).

Figure 1.1 Orla is motivated to try out her new climbing skills at every opportunity.

Spontaneous movement play

What Archer and Siraj are describing is the way that the spontaneous movements children make as they play are instinctively triggered in response to developmental processes. They describe how this includes physical activity, but is also much more than just running around or doing PE. It is impossible to engage in any kind of physical play without moving and, as Connell and McCarthy point out, 'Play is nature's movement motivator' (2014:212). This is the case whether it is encouraging fine motor manipulation of fiddly building bricks and tiny people and their accessories, or gross motor movements involved in running around, jumping and climbing, or building dens and fighting monsters. Structured movement has its place, in ring games, PE sessions and other adult-directed activities – but it is not driven by the same individualised programme of specific movements and relevant repetition that is triggered within each child's brain, when they are allowed the space and time to develop their own play. Hannaford stresses that it is 'voluntary' movements that matter. She comments 'Self initiated movement, exploration, interaction and physical experience for the joy and challenge of it, facilitates neuro-genesis (nerve growth) for a lifetime' (Hannaford 2005:22).

To be most effective in brain/body development, movement play needs to be spontaneous and driven by the child. Imposed and prolonged periods of intense activity are NOT what we are talking about here. The kind of activity that best supports young children's development comes in what Linda Pound calls 'self-chosen bursts' (Pound 2013:7) and is 'the kind of physical activity or movement play in which children engage throughout their waking moments – given half a chance!' (Pound 2013:6).

HAVE A THINK ABOUT... THE KINDS OF PLAY CHILDREN ENGAGE IN SPONTANEOUSLY

What differences might you see between the spontaneous movement play of two-year-olds, three-year-olds, four-year-olds and five-year-olds?

Why has physical development been ignored and underrated?

Let's look at some of the reasons why physical development may have been neglected in recent times and considered to have less importance than other areas of 'cognitive' development or academic skills.

■ Firstly, we tend to take it for granted. As described earlier, children's bodies generally grow and if they don't, it's regarded as a medical or child protection issue, related to nutrition and general care. It is true that we have seen a recent increase in emphasis on the role of physical activity in reducing obesity, either in children or in the later adults they will become, but as Angela Nurse pointed out in 2009 in her book *Physical Development in the Early Years Foundation Stage*, 'the centrality of good physical development to other areas of human functioning does not seem to have been taken fully into account' (Nurse 2009:6).

■ We also tend to take it for granted that children enjoy movement – so much so that we spend a lot of time focusing on getting them to be still – and we make value judgements based on their ability to NOT move. Children soon learn that not moving can earn them praise – and the best 'jobs', a place at the front of the line, or even served first for dinner!

■ Finally, it is impossible to ignore the current 'disproportionate emphasis' (Nurse 2009:7) on top-down target setting for cognitive development and the academic skills of literacy and numeracy, linked with a lack of physical development training for teachers and practitioners working with young children. This has led to the 'disembodied education' described by several commentators (e.g. Walsh 2004 and Tobin 2004) that focus purely on the brain and not the body. This is despite the 'holistic' nature of many approaches to early childhood education, that list physical development along with social, emotional and intellectual development as key areas of focus for the development of the 'whole child'.

■ Physical exercise is regularly seen as a task or lifestyle choice rather than as part of everyday experience (Goddard Blythe 2005:3). This might be as a result of our increasingly sedentary lives, but it has also been driven by the commercialisation of health and fitness and the assumption that it is something one 'ought' to do, ideally wearing specific clothes and with the help of a DVD, gym membership or even one's own personal trainer. Similarly, the separation of PE from the rest of school activities has made sure that the development of body and mind are also separated, as though the mind is developed in the classroom and the body through a PE lesson (Boorman 1988, cited by Bilton 2002:109).

Disembodied education

Joseph Tobin, writing in 2004, suggested that:

> the body is disappearing in early childhood education. Once a protected site within the larger world of education in which the body could flourish, pre-schools are now a battle-zone in the war against the body, sites where the bodies of children and the adults who care for them fall under increasing scrutiny and discipline.
>
> (Tobin 2004:111)

He describes how very young children are spending less time playing in the sand than they do at the computer, that their teachers and carers feel less free to offer them a hug or to sit them on their lap, and that they are generally discouraged from affectionate or energetic contact play with each other. He believes there are several causes at the root of this. These include:

■ **Moral panic** as a result of increased anxiety about paedophiliac behaviour. Tobin is clear that 'In this climate of panic and accusation, not only teachers but also young children are criminalized: play that in other eras and other cultures would be considered normal and unexceptional becomes evidence of them being victims or perpetrators of sexual crimes. Viewing the actions of early childhood educators and young children through a lens of potential sexual abuse leads to the imposition of draconian, wrong-headed solutions which themselves create new problems, impoverishing the lives of children and teachers' (Tobin 2004:112). Children seek attachment through physical contact

— adults bond with children through that same physical connection. One of the special joys of caring for and working with children is to share in their exuberant physicality and to share affectionate touch and holding. But a lot of carers are now so overly anxious about safeguarding themselves as well as children that we are in danger of creating a touch-deprived environment with disastrous results for all children, but particularly those for whom home (for whatever reason) is also a place where affectionate touch is lacking. He also writes of increased concerns about children's sexually explorative play (which previously might have been considered as healthy childhood curiosity) and concerns about HIV and transmittable diseases, which, although valid, can be overplayed in an early years environment. Tobin is writing about the situation in the USA, but it is not too difficult to see that this root cause, as all the others, could easily apply in the UK and elsewhere in the world.

■ **Logocentrism,** which Tobin sums up in the phrase 'Use your words' (Tobin 2004:117). His concern is that there is a greater emphasis on young children's verbalisation of their feelings and emotions at a very young age, requiring them to access higher centres of the brain than they are readily able to do in order to 'translate' and explain their feelings to adults. He fears this can lead to a denial and downgrading of the natural instincts children have for expressing themselves physically.

■ **Government initiatives and pressure for academic achievement earlier and earlier.** Tobin comments on the American 'No Child Left Behind' initiative, remarking on the way that it increased the provision of pre-schools but 'only if those pre-schools emphasize academic over social development'. In particular, pre-schools were ordered to use phonics programmes to teach early reading. Similarly, in England, pre-school provision has multiplied, is often targeted at vulnerable families, but has an emphasis on academic attainment and phonics teaching, leading to a phonics test at age six. New plans for Baseline Assessment to be carried out in the first term of the reception year (midway through the Early Years Foundation Stage) currently show little or no acknowledgement of the crucial contribution of a child's physical development to their learning and achievements.

■ **Brain research** leading to a 'hot-housing' approach to early education programmes that reduce 'playground time and social play in favour of "brain rich" activities teaching pattern recognition, numbers and phonics' (Tobin 2004: 122). Whilst agreeing wholeheartedly with Tobin's opinion on the damage done by focusing too readily on the cognitive, we would argue that there is a basis for using neuroscientific information in a measured, thoughtful way that provokes reflection and validates child-centred practices, enabling practitioners and parents to appreciate the 'why' of early learning as well as the 'how'.

Tobin (2004) believes that all of these reasons for an increasing disembodiment in our early childhood settings are linked by a common focus on 'rationality, control and risk avoidance. Collectively, they suggest the need for order, policing, discipline and surveillance' (Tobin 2004:124). In the way that an inexperienced practitioner might seek to keep children from doing anything risky and challenging, by keeping them close by, sitting at tables with closely monitored worksheets, governments also seek to control early childhood education with the initiatives and curricula that their limited understanding allows, falling back on the methods and ideology used to 'educate' and control the masses since Victorian times. Meanwhile, an experienced practitioner, confident and relaxed, can allow children the freedom to take risks, to challenge and to stretch their wings, safe in the knowledge that they have the skills to deal with situations as they arise and an understanding of children and their development that will support their judgements and actions.

Sir Kenneth Robinson also commented on the dangers of 'disembodied learning' in his TED Talk (2006) entitled *Do Schools Kill Creativity* when he stated that 'as children grow up we start to educate them progressively from the waist up, and then we focus on their heads, and slightly to one side' (Robinson 2006).

Embodied education

Other commentators concerned about this trend include Daniel J. Walsh who, like Tobin, has researched the differences between attitudes towards children's physical development across cultures. He noted that in Japan 'young children are viewed as essentially and importantly physical' (Walsh 2004:97) and that their physical development is central to their early schooling. He cites Japanese early education specialists who believe, much like Goddard Blythe and others in the UK, that 'intellectual development requires a balanced body and that physical play aligns the body' (Harada and Saito 1997, cited in Walsh 2004:97). His experience of Japanese pre-schools is that, compared with contemporary American pre-schools, they are 'raucous places, filled with loud, rambunctious kids who run, wrestle, hit, roughhouse and climb on and over everything' (Walsh 2004:99).

Principles and programmes

In her article 'PD: Principles into Practice' (2015), Dr Lala Manners draws our attention to another perspective on physical development and its role in early childcare and education. 'Central to mid 20th century pedagogical thinking, PD was never considered as separate from other areas of development. It underpinned and informed all learning and was only obliquely linked to general health and mental wellbeing' (Manners 2015b).

With the arrival of the Foundation Stage in England in 2000, however, physical development took its place amongst the six Areas of Learning. In 2012 another major shift in curriculum and policy for early years provision occurred, with the decision to divide the areas of learning into two – the Prime areas and the Specific areas. There are several positive aspects to this, as we will discover, but, as Dr Manners reminds us, this subtle shift brings with it 'goals' and assessment demands that have led to 'programmes' for physical development that focus on the 'acquisition, rehearsal and refinement of skills /competencies through a sequential syllabus of work' (Manners 2015b). Like Dr Manners, we agree that the 'principles' and 'programmes' approaches are not mutually exclusive, but we also agree with the eight key principles that should underpin our appreciation of, as well as our approach to, children's physical development.

Principles

A principles approach has the drawback of requiring 'more time, patience and confidence of the practitioner' (Manners 2015b), given its indirect and implicit style of teaching. However, it is more likely to ensure that physical development is embedded in daily practice, encouraging and enabling self direction and discovery together with positive behaviours and dispositions that are considered just as important as the skills and competencies acquired.

The eight guiding principles are:

- Movement is the primary means by which concepts are experienced.

- Start where the children are: build on their previous whole-body experiences that promote their natural growth and development.

- Use the immediate environment as a learning aid.

- Use music and rhythm as a learning aid.

- Group and teamwork aids the development of the individual.

- PD skills are transferable and should have meaning in all aspects of a child's life.

- PD apparatus should be accessible and manageable, with open-ended outcomes and readily available.

- A 'canopy' learning experience is promoted that includes free and structured play as well as specific adult-led PD sessions.

(Manners 2015b)

Practitioner training

Key to practitioners' ability to work with these principles rather than 'deliver' a programme, is the quality of initial training and continuous professional development they receive. It is to be hoped that the acknowledgement of Physical Development as one of the Prime areas of the EYFS will ensure greater input for students and trainees as well as ongoing support for practitioners, including childminders and those working with vulnerable families. Just as crucial is to ensure that awareness is also raised amongst teachers of older children, and senior leaders and managers in education, childcare, play work and youth and community work of the nature and relevance of the Prime areas to children's later development.

More than skin and bones?

'Children's minds live in their bodies, so the two are inseparably interlinked' (Nurse 2009:6).

But is there a Prime area that is more Prime than the others? The fact that this is such a tricky question in itself shows just how fundamental these three areas are to life. Emotional health and the ability to make and sustain social relationships are of course vital, not just to the individual, but to society itself. Communication and the development of speech (in one or more languages) are again fundamental to our social life and to our wellbeing and understanding of ourselves and the world in which we live. But it is an undeniable fact that all of the above don't actually mean much if we don't have a physical body in which to house them. However, as we endeavour to explain throughout this book, physical development is about so much more than just the skin and bones, muscles and joints of the physical body.

'New' understandings

McMillan sisters

When the McMillan sisters set up their nursery school in 1914 (Jarvis 2013) they were very clear about the links they believed existed between 'healthy bodies' and 'healthy minds'. The original 'baby camp' (subsequently named the 'Rachel McMillan Open Air Nursery School') had a strong focus on the outdoors and 'fresh air', in an attempt to improve the health and wellbeing of children living in crowded and often squalid urban slums. Physical health was important for other early years pioneers too, who emphasised the benefits not just of fresh air, but also of vigorous and energetic movement. As Helen Bilton describes in her book about the importance of outdoor play in the early years, 'The fresh air, the physical activity and the space ensured that the children did indeed become healthier' (Bilton 2002:26). This instinctive sense that children's physical development was crucial came long before any neuroscientific evidence of the links between the body and early brain development.

Education and movement

Even earlier than the last century there were other pioneers, some from education and others from a movement discipline, who were exploring these links. Pestalozzi, Froebel and Steiner all emphasised the value of physical activity and the outdoors in their philosophies for early education. In more recent times, organisations such as Jabadao and Active Matters in England, Moving Smart in New Zealand and Gymboree in Australia have promoted the importance of physical development and movement play for children's emotional wellbeing and learning development.

Diagnostic and remediation approaches

Others, such as Harald Blomberg (Rhythmic Movement Training) have developed diagnostic and remediation programmes as a result of their exploration of the links between the early spontaneous movements of babyhood and later motor abilities and brain maturation. Bette Lamont (Neurological Reorganisation Therapy) in the USA and Sally Goddard Blythe (Institute for Neuro-Physiological Psychology) in the UK are names associated with clinical approaches for treating neuro-developmentally based challenges in children and adults, approaches which have arisen from the greater understandings we now have about these links.

Health warning

Despite developments like these, and a growing body of knowledge and understanding, children's physical development has continued to lose out to the increasing emphasis on disembodied education, or 'head learning'. This is not to suggest that we would want to see a 'hot housing' approach to children's physical development, where babies are being 'taught' how to crawl properly and children forced to do tummy time to improve their baseline assessment scores. Nor do we want to see parents blamed for their failure to encourage crawling or for carrying their child in a car seat. Neither do we advocate non-clinicians making diagnoses on the basis of reading a few books about physical development.

We would hope that a raised awareness among practitioners of the value of early movement experience would increase their willingness to ensure that the learning environment provides as much opportunity as possible for children to explore and revisit in both spontaneous and structured ways those crucial early movements that support all later healthy development.

Partnership with parents

There are several key issues to bear in mind when sharing general information about physical development with parents:

■ **No blame.** We all know how unsettling it can be to hear new information that challenges your previous understanding and practice. Receiving new information about important aspects of physical development that challenges your preconceived views (or makes you think about something you had never even thought about before) can shake your confidence in your role as practitioner or parent and for some this will lead to feelings of guilt or embarrassment that they 'didn't do the right thing' and are to blame for any future problems. In this context blame is not acceptable, nor will it necessarily lead to a change in practice or future behaviour. **Remind parents we all do the best we can with the information we have at the time.**

■ **Keeping an open mind.** Our responsibility is to shift our practice in line with new information, bearing in mind that new understandings can constantly bring forth more and more information, some of it conflicting. Help parents to understand, by making sure YOU understand it yourself first so that you can explain it with observations that are relevant to their own child.

■ **Provide reassurance.** Some parents will need reassuring that a shift away from 'academics' at an early age is not harmful to their child's future achievement. Help them to understand the 'science' that underpins physical development and its links with all areas of the curriculum. Similarly, make sure they don't feel they have to 'push' physical skills and competencies before their child is ready.

■ **Family learning.** Consider creating 'stay and play', dance or movement sessions, which include family members. Look for opportunities to link with elders in the community to use their interest and experience to promote movement, dance rhythm and music sessions etc. Many of the issues regarding children's lack of movement activity are also evident amongst older people, leading to health and other issues. Combine the two for everyone's benefit!

Partnership with professionals

Most early years practitioners now see themselves as part of a multidisciplinary field, working alongside other settings and schools to promote effective transitions and liaising with other agencies to support children and their families with a wide range of issues.

■ **Ensure that you share your physical development assessments and observations with other professionals,** highlighting if necessary why you think they are significant and their implications for all round development.

■ **Make contact with other services and clinicians** who can help provide training as well as assessments and guidance for children for whom you have concerns.

■ **Consider ways you can join with other settings and agencies** to provide training for your own practitioners, for those in the locality, for those working with older children as well as for the parents of your children.

■ **Consider developing regular adult movement/dance sessions** to promote practitioner confidence in their own physicality. Ideally focus on pleasure rather than exercise!

Summary

■ Physical development has always been central to early years pedagogy, but a range of pressures have led to a perceived 'disappearance of the body' in early childcare and education and a lack of understanding about the importance of physical development.

■ Neuroscientific advances, together with general concerns about obesity, have heightened awareness, but a principled approach, supported by the creation of the EYFS Prime areas of learning, must underpin pedagogical responses ensuring that physical development and movement play are once again embedded in the daily life of children and the people who care for them.

■ Growing understanding about the links between movement play and the development of the brain challenges some preconceptions about early development, urging us to engage more emphatically with children's spontaneous physical activity and provide environments that can compensate for shortfalls in experience.

■ A shift in awareness mustn't bring blame for actions or practices in the past, particularly not towards parents. Sharing information and increased understanding can improve children's experiences, but also helps explain issues relating to physical, emotional and cognitive wellbeing that may develop at a later stage.

Implications for practice

A raised awareness of the nature of how 'the body' has disappeared from our understanding of early years pedagogy prompts us to consider what we can do to challenge this 'disembodied' approach to early childcare and education.

This will involve the provision of:

■ An environment that promotes and supports open-ended, spontaneous movement play geared to the developmental needs of individual children.

■ Staff who are trained and knowledgeable in the principles of physical development, keeping up to date with new information and guidance, and responsive to children's developmental needs through both structured and open-ended provision.

■ Information sharing for parents to ensure they appreciate the particular importance of their child's physical development and its links with learning and wellbeing, both in the early years and later in life.

■ Awareness of how children need to move to anchor their thought and that fidgeting and fiddling with things doesn't always denote lack of concentration and attention.

■ Careful consideration of how to respond to an individual child's needs in appropriate small group times (e.g. for stories, key person times etc.) and of whether or not large group times (e.g. assemblies, gatherings etc.) are appropriate for young children and, if so, how you will support them.

Our own early experience of physical development and how it supports our role as practitioner

This chapter provides a chance to look at our own experience of physical development and the way our physicality informs our work. It also puts us 'in the shoes of the child' and helps remind us what is important about this Prime area of early learning and experience.

HAVE A THINK ABOUT... PUTTING YOUR COAT ON!

What aspects of movement do you observe when engaging in this everyday activity? For example, you might observe:

- Gross motor movements in the arms, the shoulders, the trunk.

- Fine motor movements using hands and fingers to fasten buttons or zips.

Intriguing, frustrating, compelling

For young children, whose developing bodies have different proportions and characteristics from their adult counterparts, exploring these movement possibilities can be intriguing, frustrating and compelling.

(Jess and McIntyre 2013)

Can you remember what it felt like to find a movement 'intriguing, frustrating, compelling' as a child? Let's look at these elements, one by one.

Frustrating

Do you remember the frustrations of trying to tie your shoelace? Manipulate construction toys? Use scissors? Skip with a rope? Hammer a nail on the head?

Now, how about as an adult? It is pretty easy to think of 101 frustrating fine motor activities – particularly as we get older. Trying to remove a micro sim card from a phone? Opening plastic packaging? Changing a fuse in an old style plug? Threading a needle? The list can seem endless, although most of us no longer struggle with the fine motor movements required to tie our shoelaces, even if the bending down has become an issue. Nor is it too difficult to think of gross motor movements that some of us might find frustrating – skiing or ballroom dancing come to mind – if one is not used to doing them.

Compelling

We probably all have fine motor movements that we still find compelling – clicking a ball point pen, tapping a foot, fiddling with our hair perhaps, though with regard to gross motor movements, we probably confine our compulsion to skip along the road or do a pirouette to those times when nobody is about to see us. In fact, as adults, we have probably become very good at resisting our compulsion for movements we found pleasurable and compelling as children. What movements did you find particularly compelling when you were younger?

Can you remember how it felt to:

- Roll down a grassy slope?
- Spin round and round till you were dizzy?
- Hop about on one leg?
- Slide down the banisters?
- Leapfrog over bollards, or each other?
- Do somersaults, rollovers and handstands up against the wall?
- Kick anything kickable?
- Flick anything flickable?
- Rock backwards and forwards as you listened to a story, or when you were anxious or unhappy?

We may still have the urge to engage in these kinds of movements as adults, but as a rule we tend not to, mostly because of social convention and because we have the ability to think before we act, gauging whether or not it is advisable and physically or socially 'safe' to do so.

Intriguing

Can you remember being intrigued by a new movement as a child? What kind of movements do you think five-year-olds are intrigued by? What intrigues three-year-olds or babies?

Is it perhaps harder to find movements intriguing as adults? We have lots of opportunities to be intrigued by our gross and fine motor movements, especially if we play sports, engage in fitness activities or dance, but how much do we focus on (and delight in) our daily movements?

HAVE A THINK ABOUT... THE KIND OF GROSS AND FINE MOTOR MOVEMENTS INVOLVED IN A DAILY HOUSEWORK ACTIVITY

■ E.g. washing up, ironing or folding clothes, sweeping or vacuuming.

Close your eyes for a second or two (longer if it is safe to do so) whilst you are performing a daily housework task and focus on the physicality of the activity. Notice how different parts of your body work together to achieve the task. Can you isolate just one movement in the task and then repeat it over and over again. Does the movement feel different to you now? Does it make the task any less onerous, or boring, to pay attention to the movements involved?

Have you ever tackled a routine housework task with a running commentary – as though you were a world champion 'ironer' or 'vacuumer' and the crowd was applauding your physical prowess? Try it sometime – it can make a big difference to the way you approach menial physical tasks!

Physical dispositions

What is a disposition?

Dispositions for learning have been highlighted as important by many early years specialists. Lillian Katz described a disposition as 'relatively enduring habits of mind or characteristic ways of responding to experience across types of situations' (Katz 1993, cited in Da Ros-Voseles and Fowler-Haughey 2007).

Examples include curiosity, reflection, persistence, openness, optimism, cooperation, problem solving and pleasure in learning. If the child regularly responds in a certain way then the disposition could be said to be 'robust', but it could be described as 'weak' if they rarely respond in this way.

Physical dispositions don't often get included in the discourse, however. Some definitions, as in the dispositions to be 'gentle' or to be 'boisterous', for example, are more likely to be classified as 'habits' or 'traits' (Passmore 1972). Yet Tony Bertram and Chris Pascal identify four dispositions they consider to be indicative of an effective learner:

- Independence

- Creativity

- Self motivation

- Resilience.

(Bertram and Pascal 2002, cited in
Da Ros-Voseles and Fowler-Haughey 2007)

These are all fundamental to a child's physical development and are linked strongly with their growth as a physically active human being, engaging with their environment through movement and their senses.

Environmentally sensitive

Bertram and Pascal (2002) also point out that dispositions are 'environmentally sensitive' – meaning they are acquired and supported (or weakened and damaged) by a child's environment, which specifically includes their interactions with significant adults and other children. Unlike many specific skills, most of which can be acquired later in life if the opportunity is missed early on, a damaged disposition is much harder to restore. For example, although it is desirable to learn to read and write in childhood, there are many examples of adults who have learnt the skills much later in life. Conversely, we all know older children and adults who, although technically able to read and write, avoid doing so and would never choose those activities for pleasure – the disposition to be a reader and writer having been weakened and possibly destroyed by negative early experiences. We believe that regardless of whether described as a disposition or a trait, the same could be said of a child's ability to trust and discover the world, through their physicality, their whole body and senses.

Early dispositions

Some of us will have been very aware of our physicality being dependent on the context we found ourselves in, or of a particular incident or event that changed our view of ourselves either for good or bad. However, for many of us, it was the opinion of others that was the strongest influence on our own estimation of our physical prowess. It might have been a parent, a particular teacher, a sports coach or other children who provided us with the feedback, encouragement and positive regard that left us with the sense that we were physically able and competent. Or that we were not either of those things – and though it is not impossible to shift that mindset later in life, an early negative attitude can have wider and far reaching implications for our health and general self-esteem. Writing about Japanese attitudes to physicality in both children and adults, Daniel J. Walsh observes:

Japanese kids eventually develop into the polite, quiet adults of the stereotype, which in fact, they are when the context calls for quiet and politeness. But children are expected to be loud and wild – their spirit is not to be quashed. Middle school and high school will do that, but by then the spirit will be fully formed.

(Walsh 2004:105)

His further comment that 'A mature, polite adult not informed by this spirit is an empty shell' (ibid.) reinforces this sense that a positive disposition for a strong sense of one's own physicality must be fostered in the early years, if it is to survive into adulthood.

Neural pathways

It is easy to see how dispositions or 'habits of mind' might be linked to the way pathways are created in our brains, due to nerve connections (as described in Chapter 1). Thinking broadly about learning and dispositions in terms of pathways is a useful analogy. Imagine you live on one side of a field and need to get to the other side every day for work. The grass in the field is high and to begin with you have to work hard to create a path across. But the more you make a habit of using the same path, the more you not only work out which is the quickest route, but you also wear away the grass to make your journey easier every day. In the meantime, the grass in the rest of the field grows higher and, because no one walks there, brambles and nettles grow thickly. The path you have forged gets you to work quickly, which is good, but that doesn't always mean it's the safest path. If it's raining or icy, the path gets very slippery, but you continue to use it as to forge a new path seems too hard and will only delay you. However, if for some reason your usual pathway becomes blocked, you will have no choice but to find a new way round and this might prove so difficult, exhausting, or even threatening (because of the stinging nettles and thorny brambles) that you give up and go home instead. This can also be true of our brains. A disposition to think in a certain way, a postural habit, or a tendency to always react in a particular way to a specific stimulus becomes 'hard wired' and familiar, even if it isn't always healthy or good for us. To rethink our behaviour can be really difficult and exhausting – and even threatening if it makes us feel physically or emotionally unsafe. This is what can make it so difficult to change a disposition later in life.

HAVE A THINK ABOUT... SOME OF THE WORDS USED TO DESCRIBE CHILDREN, THEIR PHYSICALITY AND HOW THEY ENGAGE WITH THEIR ENVIRONMENT

■ Boisterous. Lively. Risk-taking. Cautious. Timid. Noisy. Quiet. Skilful. Clumsy. Gentle. Rough. Attentive. Sensory-seeking. Animated. Calm. Resilient. Fearful. Un-coordinated. Self-reliant. Persistent. Exuberant. Strong. Anxious. Energetic. Careful. Quick-moving. Fidgety. Poised. Body-confident. Can't sit still. Well-balanced. Hyperactive. Ungainly. Gawky. Fearless. Robust. Bouncy. Good at colouring in. Dainty. Delicate. Flitting. Co-ordinated. Slapdash. Slow-moving. Tactile.

Are these words you use to describe children?

Are there any you wouldn't use? Why?

Positive or negative?

Dispositions are generally described as positive or negative. For example, 'openness' is a positive disposition for learning, whereas a 'narrow' or 'closed' mind is considered to be a hindrance to learning. Many physical traits, however, can be seen in both a positive and a negative light, depending on context, although some terms such as 'lazy' and 'slow' have very negative connotations. Words such as hyperactive (and its colloquial abbreviation of 'hyper') have also become very loaded with negative implications, although their clinical use is just a description of the level of activity – with the corresponding (though much less used) word 'hypoactive' to indicate under-activity.

However, what if we didn't consider them in terms of positive and negative? Many of these traits are just the flip sides of each other. Look at them again and see if there are any obvious pairings. Perhaps we should be seeking balance for our children in that they are able to access either 'side' of the disposition depending on need and context? If that's the case, then what do we need to do to foster and support this balance in order to enable children to:

■ Build on their healthy sense of caution ... but learn it's ok to take risks sometimes?

■ Keep taking risks ... but learn the value of caution?

■ Retain their gentleness ... but explore how it feels to be vigorous?

■ Take delight in their vigour ... and develop the sensitivity to be gentle?

■ Be strong communicators ... and good listeners?

■ Build on their quiet attentiveness ... and find their strong voices?

NOW HAVE A THINK ABOUT... YOUR PHYSICAL TRAITS AND DISPOSITIONS

Pick the one most likely to have been used to describe YOU when you were very young.

- Cautious

- Risk taking

- Vigorous

- Gentle

- Quiet

- Vocal

Now pick the one that would NEVER have been used to describe you!

Did you feel that those words accurately reflected who you thought (or felt) you were at that time?

Would you describe your physical dispositions differently now as an adult or are they still pretty much the same?

I wish someone had …

Use the following statements to appraise your own early experiences of physical development and activity.

For example, what do you wish someone had helped YOU with?

- Helped me to…

- Shown me how…

- Encouraged me in…

- Given me time to…

- Watched me when…

- Taught me to…

- Supported me when…

- Kept me safe while…

Responding to children

Do you recognise children in your setting who remind you of yourself at that age?

Can you complete those sentences on their behalf; with specific examples of ways you can support them?

Now what about the children in your setting who you recognise are very DIFFERENT to you at that age? How far are you able to address their needs? It is perfectly possible to empathise with children (or adults) who function in ways very different to ourselves – indeed it is very much part of our role as professional carers and educators to be able to do so – but are there colleagues, parents and other professionals with whom you can liaise, who can help provide the insights that you need to be able to support these children well? How will you observe and engage with the children themselves so that they can voice their own needs for their physical development and positive dispositions for learning?

Try incorporating these statements into your planning by giving 'voice' to individual children's needs.

- Help Jagdeep to … develop his confidence in climbing without support.

- Show Lucy how to … line up the two sides of the zip on her coat.

- Encourage Bobby in … his interest in sweeping with the big broom.

- Give Duwayne time to … persist in tying his shoelaces.

- Watch Freya when … she wants to shows off her hopping skills.

- Teach Karlo to … hold the scissors correctly to reduce his frustration.

- Support Josef when … he wants to try stepping across the tree stumps.

- Keep Amina safe while … she sets herself risky challenges on the climbing wall.

Our role

Whether as parents, carers, or educators, supporting children's physical development demands that we assume a range of different roles. We need to be:

- Coaches and cheer leaders

- Teachers and demonstrators

- Play facilitators and playmates

- Observers and assessors

- Innovators and challengers

- Movement and dance partners

Clearly, there's a lot more to working with young children than most people think – and most of these roles apply to all aspects of the job, not just supporting physical development.

But let's look more closely at some of these roles in the context of children's physical development and see how they apply to working with children of different age groups.

Adult as coach and cheerleader

The traditional image of a coach is someone training sports players to perform particular skills and improve their performance, maybe standing on the sidelines urging them on. Although this can be relevant in the early years for children playing sports or learning gymnastics, for example, we also have to ask ourselves, what could this look like in a baby room? It certainly doesn't involve training a child to crawl in a certain way, or making them repeat certain actions over and over until they have got them right. But it might involve being by the side of a crawling baby who has discovered the step leading to the outdoors and wants to crawl in and out and up and down the step over and over again. Or assisting the three-year-old who needs help getting backwards down the ladder on the climbing frame, who needs someone standing behind, guiding them how and where to stretch a foot down to feel for the next rung on the ladder, without touching or lifting them down so that they have the chance to do it for themselves. However, the coach is standing close enough behind them to catch them should they fall, so as to give them courage and confidence enough to try. The cheerleader is the adult who excitedly claps the baby crawling in and out for themselves over the step, or gives a big smile to the three-year-old climbing down the ladder on their own for the first time, praising them for the effort put into doing it by themselves.

Adult as teacher and demonstrator

The teacher and demonstrator role, on the other hand, involves showing a child how an action is performed, sometimes explicitly as in how to hold their hands to catch a ball or 'here, let me show you an easy way to put your socks on'. But demonstration and teaching can also be achieved implicitly, as in the way a caregiver talks through the process of dressing a young baby, with phrases such as 'and now I'm putting on your socks like this – I'm going to scrunch them up and then I'm going to hide your little toes in here and then I'm going to hide your foot in here and then pull up your sock and now your foot is all nice and warm!' Teaching and demonstration are not always performed at the front of the class and the above example shows how the distinction between teaching and care-giving is often blurred – as any parent will know.

Similarly, we also demonstrate or 'role model' how we pay attention to our own movements, make our own 'risk assessments' and employ patience and perseverance through physical challenges. For example:

- Carefully choosing a stool to reach a high shelf

- Persevering with a fiddly task, like tying an apron or using sticky tape to join materials

- Asking for help to carry something heavy, or to complete a difficult task

- Patiently having a few goes before being able to achieve a new physical challenge.

Often it helps to make the modelling more explicit if the children hear us use 'self talk' or 'self questioning' as we go about these challenges:

"Hmm, I think I'd better use a stool to help me get those books down from the shelf, I don't think I can quite reach by myself."

"I'm getting all stuck up with this tape, I wonder what I'm doing wrong?"

"I think I'm going to need help with this, it's too heavy for one person."

"I need to practise this some more, but I think I am getting a bit better at it."

Adult as play facilitator and playmate

Children don't always want adults to lead or direct their play, but they love having adults as playmates. Being really 'present' in children's play means focusing on them with attention and actively listening to their verbal and non-verbal communication whilst following their lead and 'going with the flow' of the play situation. Physical movement play is likely to involve touch, which can be gentle and affectionate as well as firm and powerful as in 'rough and tumble'. This is sometimes also referred to as 'cub play', which is a good way to describe the kind of boisterous and vigorous contact activity that children engage in by themselves as well as with adults. See Chapter 7 for more on rough and tumble. Playmating can also involve mirroring, where the adult mirrors the child's movement perhaps in an overt way, or, in the case of a shy or less engaged child, a more discreet copying of movement, action, facial expression etc. that allows the child to take the lead and direct the pace of play, or to indicate when they don't want to engage.

The play facilitator is not just the adult who sets up the environment, provides the resources and designs the open-ended play opportunities. They can sometimes be the adult who ensures they stay out of the child's way so as not to interfere with the play! Just as importantly, they remove hazards and barriers to children's play, supervise where appropriate, and are available for advice and guidance and to support negotiation and conflict resolution should it be necessary, ensuring as far as possible that all children benefit from the physical play experience and that some children's needs do not dominate over others.

Adult as observer and assessor

Sometimes the adult's role is to stay well out of the way, but we also have a responsibility to observe what is going on in children's physical play, both by making formal observations on occasions, or by noting significant aspects. It can be possible to make useful assessments this way, using a sound knowledge of child development and a personal knowledge of the individual child to gauge what is significant. This can then inform planning for the individual or groups of children that ensures the appropriate play experiences (and resources) are available for children's self-chosen activities that will support continued physical development and learning. The more knowledge we have about children's physical development, the better we become at assessing natural progress, recognising typical and atypical development and able to plan experiences and opportunities accordingly, to suit each child. This is what Penny Greenland refers to as 'watching for gaps' (Greenland 2000:142) and noticing 'what is trying to happen' (Greenland 2000:190). We will look more closely at assessment of physical development in Chapter 7.

Adult as innovator and challenger

The role of innovator allows the practitioner to revel in their own creativity and to explore their physicality in the way they respond to children and to the environment in which they work. Seeing the possibilities of the outdoor or indoor space, for example, to promote and encourage children's movement by creating resources, recycling equipment and encouraging alternative uses for the space or the things in it. Not only does this provide children with a greater variety of stimuli, it also shows them that innovation and creative ways of viewing the world are both possible and desirable. Being curious is an important part of this – demonstrating your own curiosity about the different ways your body can move or interact with the environment, crawling through the long grass, for example, stretching up a tree trunk or swirling circles in the sand.

The challenger role is hugely important in stimulating children to extend themselves and to have positive expectations of their ability. But it is no good challenging children if you have no idea what they might be capable of, nor of what is motivating to them. A parent or key person who is tuned in to the children in their care will know exactly the right level of challenge to pose for a child, and also the degree of support that might be required to get them there. As already mentioned, the challenger role also involves explicitly demonstrating how we challenge ourselves, perhaps with a new skill or the perseverance and physical effort needed to continue with a difficult task.

Adult as movement and dance partner

Whether or not you consider yourself able to dance, I think we all know the pleasures of twirling around and skipping along with children, especially to music. Whether the dance is improvised or is choreographed to the latest pop hit, we can all have fun joining in with the moves. Our training sessions for early years practitioners always include a mix of physical activity and theory. As the American novelist Vicki Baum (1888–1960) once said, 'There are shortcuts to happiness – and dancing is one of them!' and it is always a privilege for us to have practitioners trust us enough to kick off their shoes and get happy, dancing around to music 'as if nobody's watching'. We can't all be Billy Elliot or Darcey Bussell, but we should all 'feel at home' enough in our bodies, at any age, to be able to access the feel-good hormones that dance and expressive movement can generate.

Children appreciate adults joining in their dances and also collaborating in a multitude of other movement activities like rolling down slopes, hopping and jumping, skipping with ropes, playing 'row row your boat' or 'horsey horsey', or just lying in the grass watching the clouds. For babies, it is good to remember that you (and your body) are their first playground. Being held in your arms, lying on your lap or your tummy, dandled on your knees or carried on your shoulders, provides a baby or young child with supported movement activities that offer connection as well as valuable stimulation.

HAVE A THINK ABOUT... THE DIFFERENT ROLES ABOVE

Can you think of examples during the day when you perform these roles?

Do you think any are more important than others?

Which are you more comfortable with?

Now think about where, when and how you are most likely to fulfil those roles.

How many of them involve sitting down?

How many involve movement?

Which are more likely to happen indoors? Which are more usual outdoors? Does this always have to be the case?

Are there some roles you never feel able to fulfil? Why do you think this is?

If you work as a team, are you able to ensure that all roles are covered?

If you work alone, what support would you need to fulfil all roles?

'Tuning in' to children

One of the most significant aspects of our role as 'key people' for the children with whom we work is the ability to 'tune in' to them – to their needs, their interests and their motivations. This is particularly important with regard to their physical dispositions and competencies as well as their physical needs. Knowing a child well means we can 'scaffold' their learning appropriately, helping them with what Vygotsky referred to as 'the zone of proximal development' (Mooney 2013:101). This means recognising 'where they are at', acknowledging what they can do independently, appreciating what they need to be able to do next (or want to do) and ultimately how to help them with that task until they can do it by themselves. It is this kind of 'scaffolding', perfectly tuned to the individual child, that helps build competency and physical mastery without damaging the positive disposition to want to continue to engage in the activity.

HAVE A THINK ABOUT... LEARNING HOW TO DO SOMETHING PHYSICALLY DIFFICULT AS A CHILD

Can you remember a physical skill (other than a routine self-help skill) with which you struggled as a child? Examples might include a sporting or athletic skill, or manipulating a tool.

Perhaps it was something that you ultimately managed to do with ease or maybe it was something that you still struggle with to this day?

What (or who) helped you with it?

What (if anything) would have helped you better?

Can you remember the process of:

a) not being able to do it?

b) being helped or 'scaffolded'?

c) being able to do it independently?

Do you remember any of the feelings associated with the process of learning that skill?

How do you feel about this skill now as an adult?

Is it something you do regularly with pleasure, or something you avoid or choose not to do?

Do you think your gender made a difference to your physical skills – and to the support and encouragement for your physical development that you received as a child?

What's sex got to do with it?

Are boys and girls really very different when it comes to physical development? We have lots of received wisdom that suggests they are, despite a strong equalities agenda that attempts to challenge many of the stereotypes.

Let's look at the stereotypes first.

HAVE A THINK ABOUT... GENDER PHYSICAL STEREOTYPES

Boys are strong – girls aren't.

Girls are dainty and elegant – boys aren't.

Girls can run fast and play sport well but women will never be as fast or as athletically skilful as men.

Can you think of other examples of physical stereotyping?

What do you think of these statements?

Do you know boys and girls, men and women who contradict these stereotypes?

How might these stereotypes influence practitioner (and parental) attitudes towards children's physical development?

Our improved understanding of the way that gender bias can affect both boys and girls has challenged these stereotypes but has also sometimes led to a flawed approach based on notions that 'everyone is the same'. Clearly there are visible physical differences between boys and girls and it would be foolish to pretend otherwise – but are there also *invisible* gender differences that can affect the physical development of young children? In their book *The Cleverness of Boys* (2009), Ros Bayley and Sally Featherstone suggest a number of possible (though not prescribed) differences that can affect the physical and neurological development of boys and girls. These include:

Sensitivity to testosterone – can affect levels of aggression and competitiveness.

Size and rate of growth of the amygdala – an organ deep in the brain that helps us control our impulses. Though generally bigger in males, in some children it takes longer to develop its 'controlling' role.

Rate of growth of the hippocampus – helps memory and sometimes is slower to develop in boys.

Size of corpus callosum – divides the two sides of the brain and when it is thinner, as it often is in boys, it can make it difficult to focus on more than one thing at a time (multi-tasking) although it can also aid strong concentration on a single focus.

(Bayley and Featherstone 2009:25–26)

Although these are hormonal and neurological features that have been noted to occur more frequently in males, it is important to state that none of them are exclusive to boys. The rate at which they have an impact also differs, even amongst the same gender. What is important, however, is to be aware that the above issues cannot always be dismissed as the result of lack of effort or ability (or even poor parenting) in either gender and that a better understanding of the function of the brain, its architecture and chemistry, helps us to better understand all of our children and their behaviours.

HAVE A THINK ABOUT... GENDER PERCEPTIONS

Think of a boy and a girl you know or work with, whose physical development seems typical.

Why do you think they are typical? How much do you know about their early stages of physical development – before and after they began to walk?

How similar are they in their development?

Observe them over a period of time and note the choices they make with regard to physical and movement play. Are there activities you see them do all the time? Are there others they do less often or not at all?

What aspects of their physicality win them praise? Or get them into trouble?

How aware are they of their physical skills and prowess?

What do they want to do physically that they know they can't do yet?

When do they expect to be able to do it? Do they think they will need help to be able to do it or do they expect to just 'learn how to do it themselves'? Do you think gender plays a part in this?

How are your perceptions about boys' and girls' physical development challenged by your observations of these children and others you work with?

'Disembodied' teaching

'One of the great pleasures of being with young children is their physicality' (Tobin 2004:112).

If, as we explored in Chapter 1, there are concerns about 'disembodied' learning then we must also consider how teaching (and caring) in the early years might also have become more 'disembodied' in recent times. Strong reactions to concerns about child protection and safeguarding have sadly led to a general wariness about physical contact with children. This is despite the fact that it is impossible to care for young children without interacting with them physically and, ideally, with a degree of intimacy that helps build attachments.

Human touch is essential for emotional and physical wellbeing. (See more about this in Chapter 5). Babies and young children who are away from their families for any length of time rely on sensitive, caring touch for reassurance, for comfort and for stimulation. Dealing with children's physical personal needs (nappy changing, washing, dressing, feeding etc.) provides perfect opportunities for intimate connection focused on touch and nurturing attention. Physical contact is just as important for older children who still need and appreciate hand holding, snuggling and cuddling, gentle squeezes and bear hugs as well as 'tuned in' casual touch that cements connection and intimacy. In Chapter 5 we provide more information about how to respond to children with tactile defensiveness and other issues with touch sensitivity.

Teaching about concepts or ideas without movement, touch and physical interaction is typical of an academic 'heads only' approach to learning information and is not appropriate for children in their early years. They explore water by pouring, splashing, swirling, and learn about circles by drawing and spinning and twirling. Therefore, it is essential that lots of sensory and tactile 'hands on' or 'first hand' experiences are available to them.

Early years work is physically demanding

Although early years practitioners in general tend to be physically active in their work, we have to be aware of a growing tendency to see 'teaching' (even of very young children) as something that happens sitting down – at a table, in front of a whiteboard or in a corner on a carpet.

With an increasing number of children receiving childcare from a young age as well as government initiatives to 'schoolify' that care, there has never been a more important time to argue for practitioners to have a good understanding of the importance of physical development and the centrality of 'the body' in every aspect of a young child's life.

Now, we would be the first to acknowledge just how physically exhausting working with young children can be – and we certainly do not advocate constant movement as an indicator of good practice. Indeed, sitting or crouching down, is very often the best and safest way to get down to the level of small children, in order to be able to talk with them and to observe and listen to their conversations. The ideal play spaces (indoors and out) should always include plenty of seating so that adults can comfortably observe children without interfering in their play. It also reduces the likelihood of adults standing with their arms folded, or in their pockets, leaning against any available wall or fence as they 'supervise' at a distance!

However, the purpose of our suggestion that teaching involves movement and physicality is to give status to all the other aspects of our work that don't easily fit with formal notions of what constitutes 'teaching'. When we are allowed and encouraged to fulfil our roles effectively, working with young children instinctively involves a great deal of movement – as well as naturally occurring 'downtimes' when both adults and children are able to rest and relax with each other.

Partnership with parents

■ **Most of the reflective exercises in this chapter are suitable for using with parents,** carers and other professionals in training sessions, to help them appreciate the special nature of physical development and to connect with their own physicality and physical dispositions.

■ **Be a role model for positive attitudes towards physical activity and movement!** Invite parents to join in movement activity sessions and to share their skills and interest in sports, dance etc.

■ **Talk about and share** the physical skills and developments you notice in their children and what they are trying to figure out, physically. Encourage parents to share what they notice at home.

■ **Make the most of warm and affectionate touch** with children at greetings and home times, modelling for parents your hands-on approaches to offering reassurance and security.

Partnership with professionals

■ **Include all staff members in training about physical development and the importance of movement play,** particularly in primary schools, e.g. lunchtime staff who supervise outdoor playtimes and peripatetic PE or sports trainers who may not have specific early years training.

■ **Be an advocate for physical and movement play across all sectors,** e.g. challenge local authorities to provide and maintain natural play areas that support open-ended physical play, rather than just expensive fixed equipment.

■ **Find out about local initiatives that support outdoor play in your area,** e.g. Play Streets.

Summary

This chapter focuses on the relationship between our own physicality and that of the children with whom we work.

■ By thinking about our own childhood experiences of physical development and movement play, we are better able to 'step into the shoes of the child' and relate to their experiences and their physical dispositions.

■ Getting in touch with our own physicality reminds us of challenges we may have faced, as well the joy and pleasure we gain from being physically active and in tune with our bodies.

■ We also consider the impact of the different roles played by the practitioner in supporting children's physical development in order to ensure an 'embodied approach' to early childcare and education.

Implications for practice

An increased awareness of our own physicality and early attitudes to physical activity prompts us to consider:

■ How we celebrate and foster children's intrigue, enthusiasm and delight in their physicality and whole body movement

■ How we ensure that they have the space, time and encouragement to engage in all the compelling and instinctive physical activity that leads to strong physical development and healthy brain structure

■ Who we need to involve in order to ensure that everyone working with our children has a sound understanding of the importance of physical development and movement play

■ How we will use our knowledge of children's physical development and their growing dispositions, to inform our planning and support our assessments, bearing in mind any specific needs triggered by gender-related aspects of physical development.

3 The stages of physical development

This chapter looks at the key stages of physical development with a particular focus on movement and the developmental importance of what takes place before a child learns to walk. Throughout this chapter we will be referring to primitive reflexes and their importance – these will be explained in much more detail in the next chapter.

Milestones

HAVE A THINK ABOUT... LEARNING TO WALK

When did you start to walk?

Not all of us have information from our early life, but perhaps you remember being told about when you started to walk and maybe even have photos of the event.

Do you know when you first sat up?

Started to crawl?

Did you shuffle along on your bottom or did you crawl on hands and knees?

Perhaps you did these things earlier or later than your peers, or perhaps not at all?

A 'unique child'?

Any parent, or practitioner who works with babies, knows that there is something special about the way each unique little person tackles these major milestones. Two babies born on the same day, with similar rates of development, may not roll over for the first time on the same day. Nor will they sit up without help, begin to crawl or take their first faltering steps at the same time – there could be several weeks or even months between babies of the same age reaching the same stage of development. This is why *Development Matters,* the non-statutory guidance for the Early Years Foundation Stage in England (2012), was organised into overlapping age bands and clearly stated on every page:

> Children develop at their own rates, and in their own ways. The development statements and their order should not be taken as necessary steps for individual children. They should not be used as checklists. The age/stage bands overlap because these are not fixed age boundaries but suggest a typical range of development.
>
> (Early Education 2012)

This 'typical' range of development is based loosely around what we have come to think of as milestones in a child's physical development. These aren't exactly universal, however, as they are based largely on the work and opinions of an American physician and psychologist, Arnold Gesell, who detailed the 'norms' of development in babies and young children. His relatively small and narrow sample of observations has led to a skewed perspective on what is *normal* – and, just as importantly, what is considered to be *abnormal*. Gessell's typical child was male, white, middle class, from a two-parent family and from the minority world (that is, where fewer of the world's population live). His studies, therefore, did not reflect the way that 'cultural constraints – what is accessible and not accessible, valued and not valued' (Walsh 2004:108) also have an impact on when children achieve certain key developments that are critical to the way of life within their communities. Nor do we know too much about whether geographical conditions such as climate or terrain might make a difference to how and when children acquire certain motor skills like swimming or climbing that might be of more importance in certain conditions (Adolph et al. 2009).

Prescriptions for progress

Linda Pound in her profile of Gesell in her book *Quick Guides for Early Years: Physical Development* (2013) points out that since he provided us with a supposed example of what a typical child does (or doesn't do) at a certain stage, 'these highly detailed descriptions of norms of what some children actually do, have, however, come to be regarded as prescriptions of what children should do' (Pound 2013:21). Therefore, the so-called typical group then comes to be seen not just as a description of what *some* children do, but a prescription for what all children *must* do to be considered 'normal'.

Typical and atypical

Daniel J. Walsh warns us that 'The norms themselves become constraints that both enhance and restrict as society sets strong expectations about what children can and cannot do and should and should not do' (Walsh 2004:108).

The people who then become most constrained by these norms (after the children) are the parents who rush to ensure their babies fit the so-called norm because the sooner their babies roll (or sit, crawl, walk etc.), the sooner they will be relieved of the worry that their children might not 'meet their milestones'. They are just as constrained (and their children just as potentially damaged) by these 'norms' as are those parents who are left feeling worried and distressed because their children don't meet the norm. Rather than celebrating and enjoying the uniqueness of their own child, they find themselves anxious and doubting their own instincts.

Children *are* all different – that's why our early years policies talk so much about the 'Unique Child'. But in reality we seem to be always looking for ways in which we are not unique at all. If you don't fit in the 'normal' group then you must be 'abnormal'. The words 'typical' and 'atypical' are more helpful here as, for the time being anyway, they remove the negative connotations of being outside the norm and can be seen merely as a descriptor.

'**Typical**' describes the characteristics seen in most children's development within a fairly loose framework or range.

'**Atypical**' *for the authors* describes a different way of developing, which may – or may not – indicate, or be symptomatic of, an impairment or specific need.

Alternative perspectives on physical development

Rudolf Steiner

There are alternative ways of looking at the stages of physical development. Rudolf Steiner considers a child to be ready for kindergarten, not necessarily when they have reached a degree of physical independence (e.g. toilet trained) but when they begin to talk of themselves as 'I'. This is usually around the age of three years and is likely to link with physical maturity, though it will be individual for each child. Similarly, the child is considered ready for formal schooling only when the second teeth have come through, signifying the end of the first stage in physical development and a point at which the proprioceptive and vestibular systems are more developed (see Chapter 6). This is usually around the age of seven, which ties with compulsory school starting age in many countries, though not the UK.

Emmi Pikler

Dr Emmi Pikler's approach differs from a milestones approach in that it focuses on the child's self-initiated movements and 'values the quality of the movement, rather than the age at which the movement is acquired' (Pikler and Pap 2006:iii). Her careful and naturalistic studies of children undertaken over many years at the orphanage she set up in Budapest (now a childcare setting) demonstrated that 'a healthy infant – when raised in a stable, respectful relationship – has the inborn ability to learn to move, sit and walk without being taught' (Pikler 1971, cited in Money 2006:xiii). Her approach involved a clear understanding that the child should not be encouraged or supported to achieve any movement or postural position until they could do so unsupported and chose to do so for themselves. For example, babies were not to be propped up in a sitting position before they were able to roll over independently and then move themselves into a sitting position where the back was strong enough to support itself. She considered each child to be 'fully competent for his or her stage of development' (Pinto 2006:x) and 'that they move naturally with better coordination, more body awareness, a natural sense of uprightness and more grace than when they are "assisted" by propping, being held upright, or otherwise "helped" to sit, stand, walk or climb' (Money 2006:xi).

Magda Gerber

Magda Gerber trained with Emmi Pikler and in 1957 brought the philosophy to the United States, where she founded the organisation 'Resources in Infant Education' and was influential in educating parents and practitioners. The basis of Magda Gerber's philosophy is respect for and 'trust in the baby to be an initiator, to be an explorer eager to learn what he is ready for. Because of this trust, we provide the infant with only enough help necessary to allow the child to enjoy mastery of her own actions' (Gerber 1998).

HAVE A THINK ABOUT... HOW YOU ASSESS A CHILD'S DEVELOPMENTAL PROGRESS

Do you find 'milestones' helpful in your assessment of children's developmental progress?

What do you know about alternative ways of assessing children's development and progress and how far have they influenced your practice?

What has your own experience with babies and young children told you about the unique ways that children develop?

The development of locomotion

In her book *The Well Balanced Child* Sally Goddard Blythe explores a way of looking at children's locomotion development that links it with our evolutionary past (Goddard Blythe 2004:6–8).

'Evolutionary' stages of locomotion

First we are like **fish**, swimming in the watery environment of the womb.

Once born, the **reptilian** stage comes when we first begin to creep and crawl with our bellies still on the ground. This is when children first become autonomous in their locomotion, beginning to be able to put their will into action.

Figure 3.1 The 'reptilian' stage of movement.

As we begin to lift our bellies and chests away from the floor we move into the **mammalian** stage, when we use our arms and legs, hands and feet to crawl around. This is when children begin to move more independently (often with speed) to follow their own intentions.

Figure 3.2 The 'mammalian' stage of movement.

The **primate** stage begins as we learn to pull ourselves up to a standing position, but are dependent on our arms and hands for holding on as we 'cruise' around the furniture or hold onto others as we use our feet and legs in an upright position. It is at this stage that we start to become fairly expert at the art of falling down, mostly landing on our well-padded bottoms and often happily getting up again to carry on cruising.

Figure 3.3 The cruising stage.

We need to be confident at falling down as we move next into the bipedal **human** stage of confident, upright locomotion on two feet leaving the hands free for other important tasks. Goddard Blythe suggests that once this has begun, the brain is also left free to concentrate on other complex aspects such as communication and higher thinking (Goddard Blythe 2004:6).

Figures 3.4a Orla stands confidently whilst holding something in her hands. **b** Orla walks independently with confidence to pick up the ball.

Rushing to walk

Inevitably, the 'milestone' of taking those first few faltering steps matters a lot to parents. It is also considered a marker for general progress checks, with babies typically expected to begin to walk anywhere between 10 and 16 months. There will always be children who are early walkers and some who seem content to shuffle and crawl long past their first birthdays. We encourage and applaud a baby's first steps. It is a moment often recorded with photos and video. The age at which a child first walks is a question regularly asked in infant health checks. We know that a delay in walking might be an indicator of developmental or medical problems, though it has to be stressed that this is not always the case. Perhaps we should also be asking about the child's experience of crawling and creeping? There is evidence now to suggest that some children who walk early 'can sometimes miss out on aspects of sensori-motor integration normally entrained through the experience of crawling and creeping' (Goddard Blythe 2009:210) that may lead to developmental issues later on. These include:

■ Body awareness – personal wellbeing and self-care skills

■ Co-ordination – spatial awareness and motor skills

■ Visual difficulties – links with literacy skills

■ Neurological issues – affecting focus, attention and cognitive development.

This is NOT to suggest that we should be preventing children from walking early or making them crawl when they don't want to, nor are we suggesting that all children who don't crawl will automatically have issues. However, as Sally Goddard Blythe points out, 'The important point is to allow your baby to experience as wide a range of movements as possible; to enjoy and value each stage of development as it occurs' (Goddard Blythe 2004:48).

The reasoning behind this is that every one of those early stages contributes to brain development on the inside, as well as to locomotion on the outside.

Early stages of development

Let's look more closely at some of the physical development stages before walking and consider why they are important. We will look at the possible consequences if they are not fully experienced at the appropriate time and why this might happen. Later in this chapter we will explore some ways we can give them attention at later stages, in order to compensate for any early lack of experience.

Movement in the womb

A biological drive for movement begins in the womb when the movements of the growing foetus are important not just for building the skeletal structure but also for providing the beginnings of communication, sensory responsiveness and bonding. Some foetal movements are important in expanding the lungs and others, less easily felt, occur when the baby sucks their thumb, or stretches their fingers and toes.

The kicks and nudges a pregnant woman feels (and which can sometimes be seen externally) are often in response to some kind of sensory stimulus the baby is receiving. Perhaps the mother is having a cold drink, is changing position or has been startled by a loud noise. Kicks are most easily noticed when lying down and mothers are encouraged to be aware of any changes in kicking, as movement is generally considered to be an indicator of the baby's continued wellbeing in the womb (RCOG 2011). Connecting with the baby's movements is also an important way for an expectant mother (and others) to begin to connect with the baby and start the bonding process.

Floor-based play lying on the back (supine)

Watch a baby lying awake on their back and you will see a movement 'work-out' to match any adult in the gym! A young baby will kick their legs, wave their arms and move their head in response to a stimulus, particularly a recognised voice or face.

Psychologists exploring the extent of memory in babies have used as part of their research the fact that infants kick their legs to communicate interest in something they remember seeing before (Rovee-Collier 1999). This suggests not just that babies remember familiar objects, but that a key form of communication at this stage is through movement, directly linking the brain and the limbs.

The floor as a natural playground

When you think of it, the floor, or any safe, flat surface, provides a perfect natural playground for a baby. As parts of the body come into contact with the surface in different ways, babies are presented with a whole range of tactile experiences. As they change body position, they explore the effects of friction and gravity and begin to develop proprioception. This is the important sense of knowing where the body is in space and where they begin and end. (There is more about proprioception in Chapter 6.)

Floor-based activity on the back also provides opportunities for:

- Physical activity for babies before they are independently mobile

- Free movement of the head and neck

- Strengthening the muscles in the spine, trunk, neck, legs and arms

- Seemingly random movements that allow babies to 'discover' their arms, hands, fingers, legs, feet and toes as they come into vision and are eventually able to grasp

- Visual development as they focus on their moving body parts

- Creating strong connections in the brain as each repetition of a movement reinforces a neural pathway, building physical experiences into a repertoire of movements

- Inhibition of primitive reflexes (see more about this in Chapter 4).

Unfortunately, there are a variety of reasons why babies seem not to spend as much time lying on their backs, able to wriggle and kick freely, as they used to. The most prominent of these is the prevalence of folding buggies or strollers rather than prams or pushchairs that allow the child to lie fully flat and horizontal some of the time. Realistically, folding strollers that are light and easier to manipulate down steps and on public transport are better than the big bulky prams of old, but babies' spines need to stretch and uncurl from the natural 'C' shape they are born with. The same issue occurs when babies spend large amounts of their day strapped into car seats, sometimes staying in them even when out of the car. Some specialists refer to this as 'bucket baby' syndrome. Whilst there are obvious safety reasons for car seats when travelling, we have to look at just how long some of our children are spending strapped into these 'containers' and other seats and walking aids. This can have physiological and postural implications such as torticollis, where the neck becomes twisted abnormally, or plagiocephaly, where part of the head becomes flattened. Both of these can occur when a baby spends too much time in the same position, unable (and not motivated) to move and lift their head and neck spontaneously. It can also lead to cognitive and emotional issues due to retained primitive reflexes. (More about this in Chapter 4.)

As well as helping parents understand the importance of allowing their baby to spend time playing on their backs, there is plenty we can do to minimise the impact of too much time spent in car seats and strollers – see the end of this chapter for lots of practical ideas. Always seek the advice of a health professional if you have concerns about a child's growth and bodily development.

HAVE A THINK ABOUT... BABY EQUIPMENT

You probably won't remember yourself, but do you know if you had experience of any of these in your early life:

■ a baby walker

■ bouncing chair

■ baby swing/bouncer.

How might these interfere with the important early stages of physical development?

Remember most parents are just doing the best they can with the knowledge and resources they have at the time, so it is important not to fall into the trap of blaming parents for their use.

However, we now have information that challenges us to think carefully about the value of equipment like this.

What do you think is the purpose of bouncing chairs, baby swings, baby walkers etc.?

What advantages are there in using them? For the child? For the parents/carers?

What disadvantages might there be?

How do you help parents to appreciate all of this so that they can make informed decisions about their purchase and use?

Floor-based play lying on the tummy (prone)

Just as important as time spent playing on their backs is the time babies and young children need to spend playing on their tummies. Sometimes this is called 'prone-play' but mostly we know it as 'tummy time'. The benefits of regular supervised bursts of this activity are wide and various including:

- Lengthening the spine and developing neck extensor muscles.

- Expanding the chest cavity, allowing for deeper breathing.

- Encouraging weight bearing through the hands, which is important in developing a full palm stretch, which in turn helps develop dexterity of the fingers and strength of grip.

- Encouraging the eyes to focus and track at close range.

- Helping to inhibit the early primitive reflexes (see Chapter 4), for example those that tie head movement to the whole body (correct head alignment can only develop when the head is free to move separately).

- Encouraging cross-lateral connections, which are important for higher level brain development.

- Developing proprioception (see Chapter 6) and aiding awareness of bodily functions – helping with toilet training etc.

(Adapted from Towne Jennings 2008)

Despite all the benefits, it seems that many children are not getting enough 'tummy time' experience. It is commonly held advice that babies should not be put to sleep on their tummies in order to reduce the risk of sudden infant death syndrome (SIDS), also known as 'cot death'. This is very sound advice but unfortunately has led to a general anxiety about putting babies on their fronts at *any* time, even when they are awake. Although Pikler was concerned that babies shouldn't be placed in the prone position until they could roll over for themselves, specialists such as Gill Connell consider that circumstances have changed somewhat since Pikler first made her observations. She believes that children are now likely to spend much more of their time strapped into 'containers' that interfere with their natural development and that 'as a consequence we have many more children with poor upper body strength who flounder when later they find themselves on their tummy'. Connell also points out that the existence of the ATNR reflex ensures that very young babies will turn their head to ensure their airway is free, when lying on their tummies. (More about the ATNR reflex in Chapter 4.) This has led to her belief that short periods of well-supported tummy time are beneficial from early on in a baby's life (Connell 2015 in correspondence).

Possible implications of missing out on tummy time

Missing out on time spent prone on their tummies has a whole range of potential implications for babies and their later development including:

- Flat spots on the back of the head (positional plagiocephaly)
- Poor breath control leading to low energy

- Reduced weight bearing on the palms, causing difficulties with grasp and the later fine motor skills linked with pencil control and handwriting

- Visual and focusing problems likely to have an impact on later reading skills

- Poor bladder and bowel awareness and control

- A lack of activity likely to inhibit early primitive reflexes, which can affect all aspects of physical development and body control.

Some key points about putting babies on their tummies

Never leave babies unsupervised on their tummies. Sit with them, or better still get down low on your tummy too, so that you can make eye contact and see the world from their perspective. Begin with only a minute or two and build up gradually as they show you they are comfortable and happy.

Don't force it. If they are reluctant and resistant, don't worry; there are other ways of building up their tolerance and comfort levels. You (or any familiar adult) can provide a safe, reassuring surface to lie on. Rest babies on your lap, chest, tummy, or, with older children, along your legs as you recline or lie on your back. As well as chatting or singing rhymes this way, you can hold them securely while you stroke and tap or roll gently from side to side.

It is never too late for tummy time. With older babies and children who resist lying on their tummies, a cushion, bolster or rolled up towel under the chest and armpits can help. This works for adults too if you find it uncomfortable on your tummy. Look for ways that make it work for you so that you too can gradually build up your tolerance and not miss out on this valuable physical experience. See more ideas for playful ways of encouraging time on tummies at the end of this chapter.

Rolling over

Lying on their backs and kicking, most babies will eventually discover movements that enable them to shift and roll over. This is an 'intentional movement' (Pound 2013:16), so it doesn't happen automatically, although it may happen accidentally to begin with. Some babies will use this to change position from their back to their tummies and some may discover that a few sideways rolls over and over will help them come closer to an object just slightly out of their reach (Pikler and Pap 2006:28).

Sitting up

There are lots of seats and baby equipment available these days to 'prop up' babies before they are able to sit up independently. Emmi Pikler, who differentiated very clearly between 'natural' gross motor development and 'assisted' gross motor development, was very concerned that children shouldn't be encouraged to sit up before they could do so independently. Typically, this won't happen until after they can roll over. Connell and McCarthy are also very clear about this, commenting that, though adults may be well-meaning in their propping up of babies with cushions, or in special seats, they are actually preventing the child from learning how to do it by themselves. This isn't to suggest that they won't ultimately learn how to sit for themselves – clearly they will – but that they will be missing out on the important developmental work and effort that will have them move to a sitting position independently. This includes the core muscle strength involved in providing a stable base for the body and the upper body strength needed to support the head and to centre it over the shoulders. A baby needs to use and develop their falling (head-righting) reflex in order to gain the balance needed for sitting – and props will only interfere with this (Connell and McCarthy 2014). This might involve a bit of a paradigm shift for many of us. We need to look at the way we think we are 'supporting' children and recognise that we are probably interfering with a natural process, rather than helping, and so we need to think and act differently in the future. This doesn't have to mean leaving a baby totally to their own devices – it means instead that we support and provide all the experiences that will naturally motivate them to want to move into an independent sitting position. 'Children who get lots of floor time on their backs and tummies naturally build the strength and balance necessary to crawl and sit up when the reflexes are ready' (Connell and McCarthy 2014:50).

Aspects of locomotion

Commando crawling on the tummy

This is sometimes called creeping, and begins once a baby has learned to roll over from their back onto their tummy. The term 'commando' is now associated with it because it's the kind of movement soldiers in training do as they crawl under nets and through undergrowth, keeping their bellies low on the ground and using alternate forearms to drag themselves along. Sally Goddard Blythe explains that this kind of movement 'requires the ability to turn the head, stretch out the arm on the same side, place it on the floor and then *bend* the arm to pull the body forward while pushing off with the opposite leg' (Goddard Blythe 2009:85–86).

   This cross-pattern movement is very much dependent on the inhibition of an early primitive reflex known as the Asymmetric Tonic Neck Reflex or ATNR. (Find out more about reflexes in Chapter 4.) According to Goddard Blythe, if this reflex is still present and active at the time when the baby is ready to crawl, it will prevent the arm from bending, making it hard to pull the body forwards. As a result, the baby might try to use *homologous* movements. These are movements where body parts are doing the same thing so the baby uses two arms together to pull themselves along, trying to push with their two feet together, or just dragging the legs behind them. This is hard work and an inefficient way of moving and the baby may give up and just miss out altogether on the stage of crawling on the tummy. This means they are missing out on the early cross-patterning that will help them with crawling on all fours, and may find some physical activities difficult in later life such as swimming front crawl, or marching with opposite arms and legs (Goddard Blythe 2009). Presumably even military commandoes who didn't belly crawl as babies will find it difficult when faced with it in their training!

Crawling on all fours

Although belly crawling is the beginning of independent locomotion, it is crawling on all fours (or hands and knees) that really enables a baby to get moving! Now they can begin to explore their environment and turn 'will' into 'action'. They can follow or seek out somebody (or something) they want, or an activity they want to engage in. Just think of all those cupboards and shelves waiting to be investigated!

In her book *Dyspraxia in the Early Years* (2009) Christine Macintyre explains why crawling is so important for all round development:

- **Being mobile** helps build not just physical independence but also an important awareness of themselves as independent beings. It allows them more autonomy in being able to choose to socialise with others and engage in social play and interactions.

- **The crawling position on hands and knees** strengthens shoulder and hip muscles and, although probably wobbly at first, helps body awareness and the beginnings of a sense of upright balance. This is reinforced as one arm is raised to move forward and balance has to be maintained on just three body parts. The raised arm is involved in investigating direction and distance, which is important for understanding the position of the body in space. (Find out more about balance and spatial awareness in Chapter 6.)

- **Cross-lateral crawling action** is a lot more complex than we may think, now we are grown and can (probably) do it without much thought. The arms and legs have to work in opposition and this patterning sets up 'a template in the brain which speeds up later learning' (Macintyre 2009:7) for other sequencing actions and processes. These might include ordering numbers, understanding the way stories work (with a beginning, a middle and an end) and explaining actions and processes for working out problems and experiments. As Macintyre points out, 'a vast amount of motor and intellectual learning has been eased by children who have learned to crawl' (Macintyre 2009:7).

New perspectives on the world

A baby with typically developing attachments, who is beginning to recognise the 'secure base' (Bowlby 1988) provided by their primary and secondary carers, will be constructing a 'spatial map of the relative positions of objects and people in her surroundings' (Karmiloff-Smith 1994:79) but will always return to their secure base. Very often a young baby will stop their crawling to sit up and turn back to look at a parent or other key caregiver to check in with them. 'Are you still there? Are you still watching me? Am I safe to go this far?' Feeling secure, they will then head off to explore a little further! Andrea Karmiloff-Smith suggests in her book to accompany the 1990s television series *Baby It's You* that 'a crawling baby can cover up to a quarter of a mile in one session, going to and fro on her knees. Exploration fuels the desire for more exploration' (Karmiloff-Smith 1994:79).

This constant exploration opens up new perspectives on the world for babies and Karmiloff-Smith reminds us that this extra stimulation is also good for their general development and brain growth:

> There is clearly more to crawling than imitation. Otherwise why do babies learn to crawl in the first place? Crawling is not something they copy from adults. In fact it is an expression of the baby's insatiable drive to have greater mobility and increasing control over her body and her environment. She is now free to decide where she wants to explore and is no longer dependent on others to move her to her goals. And with greater mobility come greater intellectual demands. As the baby moves alone towards an object, she has to hold a goal in mind for longer than when she was immobile and things were brought to her.
>
> (Karmiloff-Smith 1994:74–75)

Variations to the standard crawl

Some babies start to crawl by going backwards. This is probably linked with pre-crawling reflexes that push backwards to go forwards. (More about this in Chapter 4.)

Some children do very little crawling before they begin to walk, and others develop their own variation to the standard 'on all fours' crawl. 'Bottom shuffling' or 'scooting' is the most commonly seen and, as yet, we seem to know for certain very little about why some children crawl this way. There are, however, several possible reasons that are sometimes cited. These can include: sinus pressure (which may be linked to food allergies); ear infections causing ear pressure and touch sensitivity to the hands (Clopton 2013) as well as an uninhibited palmar reflex (see Chapter 4) causing the hands to remain closed in a fist rather than splayed out. These would all make it less comfortable to drop the head and crawl on all fours. Another reflex that may be linked to bottom shuffling is the retention of the symmetrical tonic neck reflex (STNR) that, among other things, helps the upper body to move separately from the lower body. It is because of this reflex that the baby begins to rock back and forth on hands and knees and then, as the reflex becomes inhibited and less powerful, the baby is able to move the arms without the hips also moving involuntarily. Poor reflex inhibition can therefore prevent the baby from moving on hands and knees and so the bottom shuffle develops in response to the baby's motivation to move.

Right and left hemispheres

Crawling on all fours helps connect the two sides of the brain because it is integrating the two sides of the body. A baby needs to be able to intentionally alternate arms and legs in order to crawl and to be able to engage all three midlines at the same time. (More about midlines later in this chapter.) It also involves motor planning or 'praxis' as the brain has to work out what body part goes first, what has to stay still and what has to follow. This is a big development for a baby's brain because planning involves being aware not just of now but also of the immediate future – and their intentions in that future.

'... deliberate movement awakens the notion of deliberate intent' (Connell and McCarthy 2014:113).

Visual development and crawling

Crawling on all fours is important for visual acuity as the action helps to stabilise and co-ordinate both eyes together, improving depth perception and binocular focus, which will be very significant for later reading and writing.

The shift from looking at the floor (which is close to the eyes) with the head down and then looking out at something in the distance with the head up, whilst moving, helps develop both short and long vision and the ability to switch between the two.

Does it matter if a baby doesn't crawl?

There would seem to be enough evidence to suggest that it probably does make a difference if a baby doesn't crawl on all fours. There is a flip side to all those positive benefits of crawling. If a baby bottom shuffles or doesn't spend much time exploring crawling before (and after) walking, then it is likely that those benefits will be less available. Midline development may be compromised along with the ability to move the upper body separately, or one side of the body separately from the other. This can have an impact on sports ability as well as self-help skills (e.g. getting dressed) and, ultimately, literacy skills (e.g. moving the writing hand across the midline in order to write from left to right). It may also have an impact on 'praxis' – the facility for motor planning that enables smooth, co-ordinated movement. Visual development could be affected, as could stereoscopic hearing.

A paper published in 2013, highlighting a correlation between children with poor stereopsis (depth perception) and reduced literacy skills, noted that bottom shuffling was a factor associated with poor stereopsis (Ponsonby et al. 2013).

What to do if a child doesn't crawl

What we don't do is make the poor child crawl, or prevent them from standing or walking if they have the urge to do so independently! Nor should parents be made to feel blame, shame or guilt if their babies aren't crawling in the conventional way. This is very important. Parents have enough to deal with and information about the importance of crawling is there to support them, not make them feel more anxious or intimidated. It might be worth checking that there are no sinus, ear or other problems affecting the child's inclination to put down their head to crawl. Also consider whether the child has not yet had enough opportunity to inhibit the STNR reflex, which will be preventing them from moving their upper body separately from the lower body. See below for playful ideas for supporting crawling and remember that, even after the child is walking, there is still value in encouraging lots of crawling, which can help 'fill in the gaps' for children who didn't crawl or who were bottom shufflers. It has been known for some children to only crawl after they are already walking. It is important not to see this as a regression, but rather the child knowing what they need to do for their healthy physical development. Although some ideas may seem age-specific, they can also be adapted to suit children at most stages of development within the EYFS and even beyond. Use them spontaneously, responding 'in the moment' to what your observations tell you about a child's developmental readiness, as well as in short bursts of structured activity in small groups, if and when appropriate.

Cruising the furniture

An important next step for most children is the urge to pull themselves up onto their feet and use the furniture (or an adult's legs) first to stand (and maybe wobble) and then to 'cruise' along, stepping sideways. Increased strength in their muscles enables them to do this as well as a strong drive for independent locomotion and the chance to get to things that were previously out of their reach. The hands and arms are also important here, for holding on and maintaining stability. Babies who can't walk unaided yet can also get around by pushing something stable, like a little trolley that moves ahead of them as they push on the handle and step forward. They might also embark on their first 'mountaineering' activity by pulling themselves up to climb onto the sofa, and the desire to scale every baby's version of Everest (the stairs) is likely to start around about now. Along with learning how to pull themselves up, they are also finding out how to get back down again from a cruising position and the swiftest and most effective way is to stick out their bottom and fall back onto it (Karmiloff-Smith 1994:85).

Standing and falling

Goddard Blythe cites Barsch, who refers to babies as 'terranauts' learning how to deal with gravity in just the same way that astronauts learn how to manage weightlessness (Barsch 1968, in Goddard Blythe 2004:175). For a baby, being able to stand without holding onto anything is, when you think about it, an amazing feat, involving muscles, joints, balance, concentration and bravery!

It's important to remember, though, that 'falling' isn't just the absence of balance and a failure to stand steady – it is a very important part of the developmental process and a skill that we would do well to retain all our lives. However, unless we happen to be a contemporary dancer or a stunt person, we tend to lose the art of falling safely, which is likely to become a much more significant issue in our senior years, when falls are not only more likely to happen but also more likely to result in broken bones that don't heal so well.

At Primed for Life Training Associates, we are increasingly seeing the work we do with young children as having value and benefits for older people too; and we look forward to the development of more intergenerational work, which acknowledges the physical and emotional benefits for both ends of the age spectrum (and the middle ages too!).

Walking

Once a child has begun to take those first faltering steps it is common for adults to hold them by one or both hands with the child's arms stretched upwards. This raises the child's shoulders and can limit movement. Some physical therapists encourage, as an alternative, holding the child around the waist or under the armpits, though this necessitates the adult being low down on the floor and isn't therefore always possible or realistic. Just be aware, though, of how often you lift a child's arms in this way, so, if you can, look for opportunities when you can comfortably get down on the floor and support their walking in other ways.

Emmi Pikler describes the process when a child begins to step freely, but isn't walking well yet:

> The child walks insecurely, generally with a wide-based gait, balancing with his arms, proceeding forward by taking very small steps. His attention is focussed on maintaining balance as he walks. The arms play an important role in balancing. Initially, he may even hold onto a toy as he walks, seemingly grasping it for support.
>
> (Pikler and Pap 2006:115)

The 'terranaut' is learning how to manage gravity and at this stage, the child's entire focus is on the movement and staying upright. But as confidence, agility and physical mastery grow, then walking becomes something we can all do automatically, leaving our brains free to think, to speak and to co-ordinate other bodily actions at the same time (e.g. looking at our mobile phones!).

It is worth remembering that walking, like a lot of early aspects of locomotion, is not something that a child learns through 'training' or by copying adults. Though they will see others walking all around them, the drive to do it for themselves comes instinctively from within, not from external motivators. Which is why there is no value (but potential harm) in pushing a child to walk before their unique body is ready to do it at their unique pace.

And once they are driven to walk for themselves, they are likely to be driven to practise it endlessly and it is important we give them that opportunity. It has been suggested that 'new walkers will clock up around 9000 steps a day' (Adolph 2002, cited in Pound 2013:17) and, unless we get in their way and prevent them, they will do this easily in their infancy as they go about their business of being walkers who are curious about their environment.

Gross and fine motor development

Gross motor skills

Walking and running (and some other motor behaviours) are described as 'phylogenetic' gross motor skills. This means they 'emerge naturally as the child matures' (Maude 2001:16). Behaviours that are influenced by learning and the environment are known as 'ontogenetic'. These include cycling, swimming and other gross motor skills that rely on input (whether direct or indirect) that capitalises on the physical maturation and experience that has gone before, leading to what Maude calls 'the moment of readiness' for acquiring a new skill (Maude 2001:16). Each skill develops in roughly three stages (Gallahue 1989, cited in Maude 2001:16). First comes the *initial* stage, when the child is clearly uncoordinated and may stumble or fall whilst attempting the movement, but will probably carry on regardless. Next comes the *elementary* stage, where the skill becomes more developed. Finally, the child reaches the *mature* stage, when the skill is efficiently streamlined and co-ordinated.

Fine motor skills

There is a natural order to the development of motor control (Connell and McCarthy 2014:135). As we mentioned earlier, development is happening from the head to the toes (cephalocaudal) and from the inside out (proximo-distal).

> This order of priority, established by the brain, ensures that the large muscles necessary for coordination and locomotion are well developed first. They can then support the complex mastery of the small muscles. The hands alone have more than 60 muscles, dozens of bones and hundreds of ligaments and tendons. So you see, on the development timeline, the hands (and feet) come last.
>
> (Connell and McCarthy 2014:135)

A word about handwriting

This is important to remember when the pressure is on to develop handwriting (a fine motor skill using the hand, fingers and wrist) at an age when gross motor control is still developing. As highlighted in our introduction, long before the body is ready to enable the hand to hold a pencil in a pincer grip and judge the right amount of pressure to use to make a mark (but not break the pencil or rip the paper), it needs lots of opportunities for 'whole-body learning' to build strength in the upper body and flexibility from the shoulders down to the fingertips. As Connell and McCarthy point out, playing on the monkey bars, with all the opportunities they provide for climbing, hanging, swinging, twisting, turning and dangling, makes for the perfect exercise for supporting handwriting (Connell and McCarthy 2014:136)!

Co-ordination and the midlines

Nerve pathways

Young children need lots of physical play to support their co-ordination and movement precision. It's not just practising a new skill, it's also the opportunity to 'embed' or reinforce the nerve (or neural) pathways from the brain to the muscles, so that the messages from the brain get to the muscles more quickly and more efficiently, as we talked about in Chapter 1.

Midlines

Movement organisation around the midlines is also very important for co-ordination. The midlines are three invisible lines that divide the body up into sectors. They separate the body:

- From left to right
- From front to back
- From top to bottom.

It is the process of midline development that allows for increasingly sophisticated movement patterns as the child grows, and it isn't fully complete until between the ages of seven and nine or even older (Connell and McCarthy 2014). Developing midlines helps children isolate various body parts so that they can move them independently, but increasingly as the body matures it also enables the child to co-ordinate multiple body parts at the same time. As a result of all this midline activity, the brain is constantly building and reinforcing new pathways, particularly those that cross the midline of the brain – the corpus callosum.

The midlines develop through physical activity and there are four complete movement patterns that are important for midline co-ordination, as Connell and McCarthy (2014:114) describe:

Bilaterality – mirrored movements where one side of the body does the same as the other side. Think of the baby who waves 'bye bye' with both hands rather than one. This is an important stage in a baby's initial physical development as it enables the brain to develop evenly on both sides, although it becomes less useful when the child needs…

Homolaterality – to be able to move one part of the body whilst keeping the other parts still. So, gradually, they are able to wave goodbye with just one hand and, much later, they are able to write with one hand whilst keeping the other hand still. Imagine the difficulty of writing if the other hand can't assist in holding the paper or is fidgeting about? When it comes to crawling, however, a baby needs…

Laterality – where one part of the body can do something in the opposite way to another part. This involves all three midlines working at the same time, which reinforces our appreciation of crawling as a major brain building activity. When the time comes to use the arms and legs to cross over a midline then the child needs…

Cross-laterality – which is the most complex of all the midline movement patterns. It not only enables more complex movement, it also 'supercharges' the reinforcement of neural pathways across the corpus callosum. Mastering the control of your own body comes before being able to make sense of right and left and directionality outside of the body. As Connell and McCarthy point out, 'If a child hasn't mastered the sides of his own body, the brain simply isn't ready yet to translate the concept of "sides" to other things' (Connell and McCarthy 2014:114). This might be true of a child who confuses a 'b' for a 'd' because they can't yet 'feel' as well as 'see' which side of the line the loops should go. Often this would be seen as a writing difficulty, to be corrected with lots of handwriting practice. A more effective way of helping the child might be to provide lots of playful opportunities that encourage complex midline movements.

Self-help skills and using tools

Early learning goals

At the time of writing, the early learning goals for physical development are:

Moving and handling – Children show good control and co-ordination in large and small movements. They move confidently in a range of ways, safely negotiating space. They handle equipment and tools effectively, including pencils for writing.

Health and self-care – Children know the importance for good health of physical exercise and a healthy diet, and talk about ways to keep healthy and safe. They manage their own basic hygiene and personal needs successfully, including dressing and going to the toilet independently.

This summons up an image of a nicely slim child, carefully wending their way to the toilet with a pair of scissors and a pencil held correctly in each hand!

More than goals

It is clear to us that worthy though these goals are, there has to be much more to a child's early physical development than this. However, there is no denying that the appropriate way to meet these goals is through physical experiences and opportunities that allow children to develop the 'body awareness' and motor abilities required above. Children learn to use tools well by having firsthand experience of using tools, but the fine motor control required to use scissors safely and efficiently or to manipulate a glue gun or hammer will not be achieved without a great deal of gross motor activity first. And when children display difficulties or weaknesses in these areas (and don't achieve the 'goal'), then it is necessary to assess not just the child's gross motor functioning but also the provision of gross motor activities available to that child, before too much emphasis is placed on their fine motor activities. Similarly, a child judged as having poor self-help skills *might* benefit from encouragement to do more things for themselves, but only with the right degree of scaffolding and support, as well as the opportunity to engage in the kind of gross motor activities that, though seemingly unconnected, will ultimately promote their ability to button up their shirt or tie their shoelaces.

HAVE A THINK BACK... TO THE CHILDREN YOU CHOSE FOR THE 'THINK ABOUT' TASK IN CHAPTER 2

How much do you know of their earliest development?

Now think about … two children whose development seems atypical although they have no physical impairments.

What are the indicators for you that their development is atypical?

Do you know of any possible causes?

In what ways are these children similar/different to each other?

What do you know about their earliest development before they began to walk?

What information might be helpful?

Is it always appropriate to ask parents for this kind of information?

How do you work with parents sensitively when you have concerns about their child's development and progress?

Who else will you need to involve to ensure parents and children are well supported to make good progress?

What strategies do you think will help encourage their development?

Partnership with parents

One of the key ways we help parents understand the important aspects of child development is to share our observations of their children.

- When we note development, or are aware of gaps or concerns, we should consider how we most usefully (and sensitively) share these with parents. Some settings have 'Wow' boards where they share children's significant achievements. Make sure that children's physical achievements are noted and encourage parents to watch out for these too.

- Most of the reflective exercises in this book can be used with parents and carers in information sessions. Look out for accessibly written articles on physical development, as well as Internet resources (video clips, Ted Talks, YouTube videos etc.) that will help parents understand their child's physical development and keep them informed about latest neuroscientific information.

- Tactfully provide parents with information about children's need not to spend extended periods in strollers, car seats, and baby 'chairs' of all kinds. Be sensitive to parents' individual circumstances and provide support while they make sense of new information that may challenge their perspective on child rearing practice.

Partnership with professionals

- Find ways to inform other professionals and staff working with older children to help them appreciate the importance of gross motor development and to recognise 'gaps' that might affect school readiness and achievements.

- Liaise with occupational therapists and other professionals across health and social services, as well as care and education, who can help increase your awareness of these issues and suggest ways to work with parents to support their increased understanding too.

Summary

The physical developments seen in the first years of a child's life are strongly linked with the development of the brain. The developmental stages that a baby goes through before walking are important, not just in achieving locomotion, but in reinforcing neural pathways and preparing the body for physical, emotional and cognitive processes to come.

Implications for practice

Understanding the processes involved in early physical development ensures that due emphasis and care is placed on the developmental stages *before* walking, to ensure that we:

- Don't rush babies to reach milestones.

- Assess movement stages for the quality of development rather than the age at which they are acquired.

- Assess the environment to ensure that children are provided with the space and time they need to fully develop gross motor skills.

- Step away from the tick boxes and checklists and begin to appreciate children's unique and individual developmental progression!

Playful ideas: to support physical development at various stages

All these activities can be adapted and extended to suit different children at different stages of development. All children benefit from revisiting early movement experiences that promote balance, co-ordination, fine and gross motor skills. Observe and collaborate with children to develop activities and continuous provision that suit their current needs. Use them spontaneously, responding 'in the moment' to what your observations tell you about a child's developmental readiness, as well as in short bursts of structured activity in small groups, if and when appropriate.

Tummy time

Tummy-to-tummy – Not all babies and children will want to lie on their tummies to begin with. Go very slow and gentle and lay them on your own body whilst singing or talking to them, gradually building up their strength and confidence.

Towel tummies – With older children (and adults) try using a cushion or rolled up towel placed under the arms, at chest level, offering support and elevation.

Tipping tummies – Support children as they lie on their tummies over appropriate sized gym balls and gently rock and tip them forwards and backwards. This works particularly well in front of a mirror so they can see you, or with someone else at the other side with whom they can make eye contact. This is helpful for building attachment too.

Talking tummies – Dedicate some time to getting down on the floor on your tummy too, for chatting and smiling eye-to-eye.

Just out of reach – To encourage reaching, moving and visual stimulation for confident tummy time babies, remember to put toys and favourite things just a little out of their reach.

Flying high – Support babies across your arm(s) on their tummies, and go for a gentle zoom. Or lie back, bring your knees up to your chest, and lay baby on your shins, facing you as you hold them by the hands or under the arms. Change the level and the tilt of your legs for a flying sensation. Good for your tummy muscles too!

Slip and slide – Tape a piece of shiny fabric/vinyl to the floor for sliding on tummies.

Creeping and crawling

Tunnel time – Creeping, crawling and slithering though tunnels is packed with benefits for brains and bodies. Try making your own with fabric over the tops of tables or chairs, or with cardboard boxes; or use your own body on all fours or just with wide legs to create space to creep or crawl through.

Up and over – Create a mountain of cushions to be crawled over by babies and little ones. Hide on the other side to provide motivation to come and find you.

Snakes and crocodiles – Get down on tummies to move around like reptiles. For older children try sticky stars, shapes or sequins on the floor to sweep up with their bellies!

Get on down – Join children on the floor to participate and share in their crawling. Kneepads (as used by carpet fitters, skateboarders etc.) help ease the strain on adult knees! To encourage eye contact, wait some distance away and encourage crawling towards you.

Crawling combos – Encourage crawling in lots of different ways and combinations. Backwards as well as forwards, sideways, fast and slow, on hands and knees or hands and feet (bear crawl).

Crawling critters – Think about how animals and insects crawl. Fun imitations to try include cats, dogs, lions, tigers, bears, monkeys, elephants, spiders, crabs etc.

Animal tails – Tuck bright scarves or fluffy fabric tails into the top of waistbands, and then, on all fours, chase each other to grab tails.

Floor play

Make sure there is always plenty of floor space as an alternative to tables for activities. Put books, puzzles, games, drawing and writing resources on the floor to encourage time on tummies and knees. Remember to use the space under tables and chairs as well as on top!

Floor dancing – Try listening to music on your backs and wriggle around to the rhythm and beat.

Slip and slide, back and sides – Shiny fabric taped to the floor can also be used to slide along on backs and sides as well as tummies.

Feeling the floor – Tape different textures to the floor (e.g. tin foil, bubble wrap, furry fabric, brown paper etc.) for babies to feel.

Fine motor skills

Dancing fingers – Improvise lots of movement games (with or without music) using the fingers, e.g. crawling up to the ceiling, dropping down like raindrops, raining on different body parts, spiders on the floor, stretching the hands open and closed (jazz hands) in different directions, shaking hands up, down, across and behind the body etc. Make even tinier movements with the fingers as though they are dancing people, jumping, kicking, sliding, twisting etc.

Puppet pals – Finger and sock puppets promote hand dexterity, through the movements required to bring them to life.

Talking fingers – Draw little faces on fingertips for conversations without the aid of puppets!

Finger drumming – On tables, tubs, tin foil and other interesting surfaces. Make sure to use all the fingers individually for a great finger workout.

Tweezing and squeezing – Enhance sorting activities by using clothes pegs or plastic tweezers to pick up small items. Look for new and interesting things that provide a challenge, e.g. paper clips, buttons, pom-poms etc. Find fun things to squeeze in your hands, e.g. bean bags, koosh balls, playdough or try gathering fabric or scarves into balls and then letting go. Try lots of different sized sponges from big to tiny (e.g. makeup sponges) in a water tray for a fun squeezing session.

4 The role of reflexes in physical development

This chapter focuses on early primitive reflexes, why they exist, why they need to be inhibited and what can happen if they are retained. Much of the information in this chapter has been drawn from *Attention, Balance and Coordination: The ABC of Learning Success* by Sally Goddard Blythe (2009), which provides a very detailed account of all primitive reflexes.

What is a reflex?

Reflexes exist because a baby has not yet acquired all the motor skills it will need for bodily control. They support the developing child right from the womb and help the body to learn specific functions or act in certain ways that will be required for survival, for delivery and for good physical development. There are lots of different reflexes, but the one thing they all seem to share is that they are 'constant' in that the same stimulus will always bring about the same response (Brodal 1998, cited in Goddard Blythe 2009).

Some of these 'reaction patterns' (Goddard Blythe 2009:45) are simple to understand, others are a lot more complex. Some we are aware of and can suppress voluntarily, others are completely beyond our control, even beyond our consciousness (Goddard Blythe 2009:31). It may be that some, like the sucking reflex, can be modified slightly, in that we know a feeding baby is able to vary the rate of their sucking in response to the mother's voice (Patterson 2008, cited in Pound 2013). Because of ultra-sound technology, we now know more about early reflexes in the womb and, because they are hierarchical and developmental, they are used in early assessments from birth onwards. Hierarchical means they relate to different levels of the nervous system, from the brain stem to the spinal cord and, finally, the brain cortex. Developmental refers to the different stages at which they develop and are ultimately inhibited and no longer active. In this chapter we will provide a brief explanation for the key reflexes, highlight what is important about them and describe what might happen if they remain active when they are no longer needed.

Types of reflex

Primitive reflexes develop in the womb and are there at birth. 'They help a baby to survive the first months of life before connections to the higher centres of the brain have become established, and they also provide rudimentary training for many later voluntary skills' (Goddard Blythe 2009:39). In the first six months of life most are generally 'inhibited' which means they lie 'dormant' and are no longer active.

But if they remain active longer than they should, they can interfere with those voluntary skills. There seem to be several ways to describe what happens when a reflex becomes healthily inactive. Words such as **integrated**, **inhibited** and **released** are often used to describe the way the reflex doesn't 'kick in' anymore in the way it used to, in response to a stimulus. This is because it is believed the reflex lies dormant – as if it is sleeping in the background, waiting until it might be needed again. **Retained**, **residual** and **uninhibited** are often used to describe the opposite and less desirable situation when the reflex is still **active** to a greater or lesser degree. Some early reflexes are useful in sports (quick reactions) and some become useful again as our bodies age. But in the main we don't want those early reflexes hanging around, because they can interfere with the reflexes and postural skills that should come next and, as we will see, they can also have a negative effect not just on our posture, but also on aspects of our learning and emotional health.

Postural reflexes begin to emerge after birth and take time to develop. Ideally, by the time a child reaches school age, the postural reflexes should be fully developed and the primitive reflexes should be fully inhibited and no longer in evidence. Postural reflexes begin with the control of the head and are linked to unconscious control of our posture in a 'gravity based environment' (Goddard Blythe 2009:41).

We mentioned in Chapter 1 that our growth develops in two ways:

- **Cephalocaudal** meaning growth from our head to our toes

- **Proximo-distal** meaning from the centre outwards.

This is also important for our posture.

Groups of reflexes

The different layers of our reflex system grow in succession, as each new group forms a kind of protective layer around the one before. This helps to prevent the more primitive ones being activated inappropriately, although if there is a gap in development then some types of stimulation can trigger a less mature response.

Withdrawal response

Our earliest reflexes involve automatic whole body reactions and are all about WITHDRAWAL away from the stimulus. Put in simplest terms these reflexes ensure that our bodies JUMP AWAY from the stimulus. They are essential to our early survival, even in the womb. A sense of them continues as we mature, finding a place in the language we use to describe our physical and emotional reactions to stimulus. Someone startles us and we exclaim 'You made me jump!' or a scary sound makes us 'jump out of our skin!' It's a short hand for the bodily reaction we feel, even though we don't necessarily 'jump' in the usual sense. The significant factor at this very early stage is that the body automatically withdraws away from the stimulus, even in the womb.

Grasp or clasp response

The next layer of reflexes is still involuntary (which means we have no choice over them) but now they include the GRASP or CLASP response. 'I hung on for dear life' might mean literally hanging on – to a rope or a cliff edge – or a more metaphorical 'grasping' and 'holding on' in an emotional sense. In a newborn the 'grasp' is seen in the palmar reflex as the baby grasps a finger placed in their palm.

Postural reflexes

The postural reflexes come last, providing automatic reactions to maintain balance, stability and flexibility throughout the whole body (Goddard Blythe 2009). We speak of someone being 'well-balanced' and able to 'stand their ground' or 'stand up for themselves'. Later voluntary and adaptive responses are based on these, as we are able to make judgements about our physical reactions to environmental stimulus.

Oh that's why I do that!

Be aware that you may recognise yourself, your partner, your children or other family members in some of the descriptions below. This can be very helpful and illuminating in understanding behaviours and reactions, and provide some reassurance about issues that may have caused concern in the past or may even continue to do so. However, this book does not set out to provide clinical advice or diagnoses for you or the children and families you work with. Further advice and guidance is available from some of the sources found at the end of the book.

What causes reflexes to be retained?

There are several suggested reasons for the retention of reflexes, some of them specific to a particular reflex and others more general. Connell and McCarthy suggest that genetic pre-disposition may play a part and that assisted delivery techniques (e.g. caesarean, venteuse, forceps etc.) might interfere with the instinctive physical actions during birth that naturally release the reflexes as they are needed. Along with other specialists, they also believe that the 'containerisation' of babies and young children and a lack of opportunities for natural movement play compound these issues by preventing or limiting the amount of physical movement that is 'nature's way of releasing these reflexes' (Connell and McCarthy 2014:40). It would certainly seem that babies benefit from time spent lying on their backs (on the floor, in cots or prams and on laps), able to wriggle and shift about, allowing the body the opportunity for movement that supports physical maturation of muscles and the release of primitive reflexes.

Primitive reflexes

Let's look more closely at some of the primitive reflexes that play an important role in our early physical development.

Some of the names for the reflexes can be complex and, to add to the confusion, are often quite similar. Connell and McCarthy provide alternative terms (2014:40–46) that are easy to remember and we have added these alongside the official terminology.

Moro reflex (startle)

This reflex was originally described by Moro (a professor of paediatrics in Heidelberg after whom the reflex has been named). Babies are usually tested for the Moro reflex shortly after birth, by lowering the baby's head (placed in the palm of the hand) lower than the level of the spine. The reflex action involves the arms opening out and extending and a sudden intake of breath. The baby freezes in this position momentarily and then the arms return across the body and the baby will usually start to cry. A range of sudden or unexpected sensory experiences, such as loud noises, lights, temperature change, coughing or sneezing, can also activate it. The reflex causes an unconscious automatic reaction first, with an awareness of what caused it only arriving a few seconds later.

The Moro reflex should be inhibited by about four months and is then replaced with a more mature 'startle response'. This still involves a bodily reaction, usually an intake of breath, a blink and lifting of the shoulders, but it also usually includes a quick scan of the environment, looking for the source of the stimulus, and then a decision about whether to react or ignore it. This is because the mature response involves higher centres of the brain, reacting to perceived threat by getting the body ready to respond, but allowing the brain (cortex) time to make a rational decision about whether or not a response is needed.

Why does the Moro reflex exist?

Like all primitive reflexes it is there, in the first instance, for our survival. Under normal circumstances, the delivery process helps prepare a baby to breathe. However, not all babies breathe spontaneously on arrival into the world and the Moro reflex acts like a 'second fail-safe mechanism to stimulate breathing' (Goddard Blythe 2009:49) if it is needed. Most of the techniques well known throughout the years for helping stimulate a baby to breathe are triggers for the Moro reflex, which involves a sudden intake of breath, followed by a breath out.

As babies, there is little we can do if something threatens us – other than react with our bodies and scream loudly until someone comes to make us safe again. The Moro reflex registers changes in the environment or in our bodily position, acting firstly to WITHDRAW in an attempt to avoid the threat and then to CLASP followed by a cry to draw attention. The first phase reduces muscle tone and effectively 'freezes' the body. The second phase restores some of the muscle tone.

How does the Moro reflex become integrated or 'released'?

A lot of stress and stimuli will keep triggering the Moro reflex, so a low stress environment and feelings of being warm and safe will help release the reflex. Connell and McCarthy describe how gentle rocking and swaying help build the sense of balance and 'the ancient practices of swaddling and skin-to-skin care makes newborns feel warm, snug, and safe, much like the walls of the uterus' (Connell and McCarthy 2014: 41).

What might happen if the Moro reflex is retained?

It is easy to see that if the Moro reflex is retained it may result in hypersensitivity and overreaction to stimulus. If the brain stem is still doing all the reacting, then the cortex isn't getting the chance to make sensible decisions about how to respond and when to ignore loud bangs, flashes of light and all manner of tactile and sensory stimulation. As the Moro is the only reflex to respond to multiple sensory triggers, that leaves a lot of potential things by which we can be startled! Worse than that, a child with a retained Moro reflex can often become so subconsciously disturbed by their sensitivity that they anticipate their reactions – becoming frightened of being frightened. This can cause them to become overcautious, particularly physically, avoiding or being sensitive to any situations or experiences that might trigger an overreaction. According to Goddard Blythe (2009:59) 'the Moro-driven child can appear withdrawn and fearful in social situations or may have a tendency to be overbearing and controlling' as they attempt to manipulate their environment in order to feel safe. Similarly, Linda Pound describes how a retained Moro reflex can prolong the 'fight or flight' reaction and that this is likely to lead to 'impulsive or inappropriate behaviour' (Pound 2013:14).

Other consequences of a retained Moro reflex might include:

■ Motion sickness, 'gravitational insecurity' and other problems with balance and co-ordination (more about this in Chapter 6).

■ Difficulties catching a ball or judging approaching visual stimuli.

■ Problems with visual perception leading to difficulties sustaining visual attention. This could be linked with dyslexia where the words sometimes appear to be 'moving on the page'.

■ Also contrast sensitivity e.g. difficulty seeing black print on white paper.

■ Sensitivity to light, sounds, touch etc.

■ Adrenal fatigue due to increased adrenaline and cortisol associated with 'fight or flight' responses to stress, which can affect the functioning of the immune system.

Impact on behaviour

Along with these physical symptoms we might expect to see certain behaviours triggered by a retained Moro reflex. It is unlikely that a child would exhibit all these behaviours and some are associated with other issues as well, but it is helpful – and often eye-opening – to reflect on how an understanding of retained reflexes can help us to better understand children's behaviours.

With a retained Moro reflex these might include:

■ General anxiety, fearfulness and insecurity

■ Dislike of the unexpected, e.g. loud noises, bright lights as well as change in general

■ Poor attention, distractibility

■ Physical timidity

■ Dislike of rough and tumble, contact sport

■ Hyperventilation

■ Poor regulation of energy levels, e.g. having only two speeds – 'on the go' or exhausted.

Sally Goddard Blythe also suggests that there are other secondary psychological effects, including a lack of confidence, that can lead to low self-esteem and a need to keep safe, either by staying cautiously within a 'controlled environment' or by using controlling behaviour to manipulate events so that the child feels safe (Goddard Blythe 2009:67).

It can also lead to 'body armouring' – having a tense muscle tone, which in turn leads to a tendency to 'hold in' emotions rather than expressing them in healthy ways. This might be linked to:

■ Strong emotional outbursts when feelings explode and can no longer be contained

■ Headaches, digestive problems and other psychosomatic complaints

■ Sensory overload in busy or new environments.

HAVE A THINK ABOUT... A CHILD YOU HAVE KNOWN WHO WAS PHYSICALLY VERY TIMID

What did this look like?

What did they not like doing and how did they communicate this to you?

How did this impact on their wellbeing – and on their learning?

What strategies did you use to build up their confidence?

Now think about a child who was very controlling, particularly of their environment and the activities they liked to be involved in.

How did they attempt to do this and how easy was it for you to recognise that 'control' was behind the behaviours?

How did this impact on their wellbeing and on their learning?

What strategies did you use to address the behaviours?

Now you know more about the impact of a retained Moro reflex (even though it is impossible to say for certain that this was the issue for these children) how might you respond differently?

It may be that you recognise yourself in some of the descriptions. What would you have wanted for yourself as a child if you had needed support to inhibit the Moro reflex?

Tonic Labyrinthine Reflex (TLR) (aligning reflex)

Unlike the Moro reflex, all the other reflexes below have just one 'receptor'. That means they originate or are triggered in just one part of the body. The TLR is a reflex that responds directly to the position of the head and the way it affects the baby's vestibular system – the balance mechanism that is stimulated when the position of the head is changed. This could happen when the baby moves their head backwards and forwards, or when the head is tilted or turned (Goddard Blythe 2009).

It is believed the TLR exists firstly in the womb to assist with the birth process but after the delivery it is there to help the baby outside the womb begin to:

■ Learn about gravity and practise balance

■ Master head and neck control

■ Increase muscle tone – so that the body is ready to potentially move or hold a posture

■ Develop proprioception.

Head alignment

It interacts with other reflexes to help with the beginnings of coordination and posture as well as head alignment. It is a very important reflex as aligning the head correctly with the rest of the body is 'necessary for balance, eye tracking, auditory processing, muscle tone and organised movements – all of which are essential to the development of our ability to focus and pay attention' (RMTI 2015). Everyone knows how important it is to support a young baby's head because they have no head control. If held in the supine position (supporting their back) the head will fall backwards if not supported and, if they are gently pulled to sitting, their head lags behind. If they are held in the ventral position (supporting their tummies) the head falls forward. When the head falls forward the body curls up as in the foetal position with the arms flexed inwards. This is the TLR in flexion. When the head falls back the body extends and the arms fall out. This is the TLR in extension. As the baby grows, new postural skills develop; they are able to lift and hold up their head when lying prone (on their tummies) and the head no longer lags behind the body when they are pulled to a sitting position. Reactions happening in the inner ear – the labyrinth – are increasingly taking over from the TLR to right the position of the head in relation to gravitational position. But traces of the TLR will still be evident in typical development, up to three and a half years of age, whenever the child is learning a new postural skill or if balance or posture is placed 'under stress' (Goddard Blythe 2009:75).

Feeding

Sometimes, the TLR reflex might be a factor in how well a baby feeds. Capute et al. (1981, cited in Goddard Blythe 2009) suggest that the TLR in extension can cause a baby to arch their back when lying in the usual feeding position in the crook of the arm. It also can cause the tongue to thrust to the front of the mouth. Both of these prevent a baby from latching onto the breast and feeding well. Some mothers find that their babies feed better if the baby's head is placed in the palm of their hand, facing the breast, with the head slightly raised and the body tucked under their arm. As well as ensuring the baby thrives well, early feeding patterns are also important in the development of the mouth and later motor aspects of speech including position of the tongue and swallowing patterns (Goddard Blythe 2009).

What might happen if the TLR is retained?

The TLR is found in newborn babies but should typically be inhibited by 3.5 years because, like other primitive reflexes, if the TLR remains active for too long, then there are a range of potential long-term effects, particularly affecting posture, balance and muscle tone, which can affect the quality of movement. A child (or adult) with a retained TLR might have difficulty simultaneously doing one thing with the upper body and a different thing with the lower. This particularly affects swimming ability (RNR 2015).

Asymmetrical Tonic Neck Reflex (ATNR) (fencing)

Figure 4.1 The ATNR reflex turns Orla's head when she is resting on an adult's shoulder.

Where the TLR happens in response to the head tilting backwards or forwards, the ATNR happens when the baby's head rotates. It is believed to emerge in the womb at the time the mother starts to feel the baby's movements. When the head rotates to one side, the arm and leg on the same side as the baby is facing also stretch out (extension) while the arm and leg on the other side bend (retraction). It has a valuable function when in the womb in developing muscle tone and the vestibular system as it 'helps the foetus to move around, to turn, and to adjust its position in response to changes in its mother's posture, to make itself comfortable, to exercise its muscles and to explore its tiny world' (Goddard Blythe 2009:81).

When the baby is born, the ATNR has another important function in that when a baby is placed on its tummy (or lies up against a carer's chest or shoulder) the head will turn to one side, ensuring the baby can breathe.

Hand-eye coordination

Figure 4.2 An active ATNR reflex is evident here as Orla turns her head to follow the movement of her outstretched arm.

Babies' early vision is very unfocused. They have to learn how to use their eyes, and movement of their bodies helps them with this. In the early weeks, a baby doesn't know that their hands belong to *them* – they are just something that comes in and out of their field of vision as they wave about in front of them. When their head turns as a result of the ATNR, their eyes turn also, following the direction of the arm stretched out before them. It seems that in this way the reflex helps train the eyes to focus.

Rolling and crawling

The ATNR is usually inhibited around four to six months after birth, but if it is retained for longer than that, it can obviously interfere with rolling over and commando style crawling. Think about what a baby needs to be able to do to roll over. They need to be able to bend their arm and leg on the same side as they turn their head. If you aren't lucky enough to have a baby around to watch as they demonstrate this, take a look at the Feldenkrais video (see More Information section at the end of the book) and watch as Baby Liv shows how it's done. If the ATNR reflex prevents the arm from bending then rolling over becomes much more difficult, or even impossible.

The arms also need to be able to bend one at a time to crawl in a commando style and pull oneself along the ground efficiently with speed. If the ATNR reflex prevents this, then the baby might try to use 'homologous' movements where they pull with both arms together at the same time. As you will remember from Chapter 3, not only is there more effort involved, this way of movement doesn't assist in developing cross-laterality, which is one of the most important benefits of crawling and is linked with reading and writing skills.

The Symmetric Tonic Neck Reflex (STNR) (rocking)

The STNR is evident for a short while at birth, goes away and then comes back at around eight months, only to be inhibited again at around eleven months (Goddard Blythe 2009). This is a good example of how these early reflexes are there to serve a purpose and should disappear when they are no longer needed. In essence, this reflex means that if the arms are stretched, then the legs will remain bent and vice versa. If the legs stretch then the arms will need to bend. Through this reflex the child is seeking to have a stabilised position on all fours. You might well see this in a baby before they crawl, when, on hands and knees, they tip and rock with their bottoms up and their face tipping to the floor in a 'face-planting' position! Some babies even sleep this way, possibly whilst this reflex is active.

In a study on the 'Effect of delivery room routine on the success of the first breast feed', Righard and Alade (1990) give us a rationale for the existence of STNR in the earliest hours of a child's life. If the mother hadn't received any analgesic (painkillers) or other medication during labour, and the newborn was immediately placed on her tummy, then the baby would instinctively start to work their way up towards the breast by flexing their arms and legs in a 'false crawling' kind of motion (cited in Goddard Blythe 2009:92). Watch the Lactancia Materna video (details in the More Information section of this book) to see this in action. As the body gradually stretches out from the foetal position in the first week, the reflex and 'false crawling' start to recede.

What happens when the STNR is retained?

This important reflex also helps to change and inhibit the TLR, ensuring that crawling is possible. Its continued existence may be a reason why some children choose not to crawl and prefer to shuffle on their bottoms. It also helps the child to pull up from sitting to standing and is very important for the quality of later posture, in both positions. A retained STNR can lead to a tendency to be round shouldered and to stand 'with the head poked forward' (Goddard Blythe 2009:97), with a difficulty in sitting cross-legged or 'up straight' and not slouching when sat at a desk. It can also affect the vertical tracking of the eyes that is very important for such diverse things as aligning columns in maths and stepping onto an escalator when it is going down (Bein-Weirzbinski 2001, cited in Goddard Blythe 2009)!

HAVE A THINK ABOUT... SITTING CROSS-LEGGED ON THE FLOOR

Why do you think that is the most common way of expecting children to sit when on the floor?

How did you feel sitting that way as a child? Was it the way you preferred to sit ... or would you have liked to sit some other way?

How about sitting at a desk? Did you slump and slouch or were you able to sit up 'nice and straight' to do your work?

Knowledge of the STNR suggests that when it is retained, children (and adults) find it really hard to sit still when cross-legged. This is because the legs want to straighten when the head is forward and the arms are bent. This also makes it difficult not to slouch with the legs straight out, when sat at a desk, writing with the arms bent. It is worth remembering that those children who 'won't' sit still or 'never' sit up straight, maybe 'CAN'T' sit any other way until the STNR reflex is inhibited, and that more movement (and not less) is the best way to help them.

Primitive tactile reflexes – reflexes triggered by touch sensations

Rooting and sucking reflexes (food finder)

These reflexes are strongly linked to each other and are important in the baby's survival. They also lead to other motor activities that are important in speech development that would not develop so well without the initial rooting and sucking reflexes to trigger them.

The rooting reflex is a response to a touch stimulus – usually a gentle stroke on the baby's cheek or the side of the mouth. This results in the baby turning their head, opening the mouth and 'searching' for something to suckle. If they don't immediately find a nipple or the teat of a bottle – and the reflex is strong – they might continue to nuzzle and 'root' against whatever is there. The reflex is believed to be at its strongest in the hour after birth when 'breastfeeding is potentially instinctive' (Odent 2002). Ideally, the birth environment will support this, allowing the baby to rest on the mother, skin to skin, and seek the breast. If, for some reason, the baby is separated from the mother (e.g. because of sickness or prematurity) the reflex will weaken and may cause feeding difficulties later. The strength of the reflex is always at its greatest when the baby is hungry, and is much less when a baby is full and satisfied.

Vision training

The rooting reflex helps ensure a baby's survival, but it also helps train other sensory systems. For example, to begin with it is touch that triggers the baby to root for the breast or bottle, combined with smell and hunger. But after a while the baby also begins to develop a 'conditioned reflex' at the *sight* of the breast or bottle – the touch reflex has helped train the baby's visual system, which has now 'learned' to associate what they see with the urge to feed. Similarly, Delacato (1970, cited in Goddard Blythe 2009:121) suggested that breastfeeding helps train the eyes for monocular vision. When a baby feeds from the left breast, the right eye and right arm are restricted and the opposite is true when the mother switches the baby to the other breast. This ultimately supports the development of stereoscopic vision as neither eye becomes favoured. When being bottle fed, however, the majority of babies are held on one side only, depending on the handedness of the carer, and a study in 2007 found that breastfed babies had better stereoscopic vision (Singhal et al. 2007, cited in Goddard Blythe 2009:122).

Suckling and sucking

In the same way, the baby is also getting lots of practice at all the motor activities involved in feeding. This includes suckling and sucking, which are not exactly the same. In *Breastfeeding: A Guide for the Medical Profession*, suckling is described as taking nourishment at the breast and it specifically refers to breastfeeding in all species. On the other hand, sucking means to draw into the mouth by means of a partial vacuum, which is the process employed when bottle feeding (Lawrence and Lawrence 2010).

We all know how a baby uses their mouth to explore, to test and make sense of their world. The motor activities involved in the rooting and sucking reflexes are linked with increased sensitivity around the mouth area. This is also important for the development of the facial muscles involved in smiling and in speech. But feeding is also an opportunity for comfort and attachment, with both the baby and the person feeding them gazing into each other's eyes and enjoying the feeling of closeness. Goddard Blythe (2009:117) refers to studies that help us to understand the importance of sucking patterns in the development of communication. A baby's first reciprocal 'conversation' or dialogue happens during feeding, when the baby momentarily stops sucking and the person feeding them talks to them and makes a movement; the baby sucks again and the carer is quiet and still until the baby pauses again. This is just like the pattern of a regular conversation where people take turns to speak and to listen (Kaye 1977). Whereas all mammals engage in 'nutritive sucking', it has been suggested (Wolff 1968) that human babies are unique in that they engage in 'non-nutritive sucking' that isn't just about food intake. The baby sucks in bursts with pauses in between which, as well as enabling the baby to 'converse', also allows them to be a passive observer of their surroundings, whilst being comforted by the oral stimulation of feeding from a bottle or the breast (Goddard Blythe 2009).

What might happen if the rooting and sucking reflexes are retained?

Chewing may be difficult, leading to a dislike or avoidance of certain foods, and there may be hypersensitivity around the mouth. Because the muscles of the mouth, jaw and tongue don't develop well, control of them remains immature, affecting speech and articulation. The link between the hands (palmar reflex) and the mouth mean that there may be difficulty talking and doing things with the hands at the same time, or that involuntary mouth movements may occur when using tools or writing etc.

Palmar grasp reflex (grasp)

Figure 4.3 Orla with evident palmar reflex.

Putting a finger in a newborn's hand triggers the palmar grasp reflex. There are two parts to the reflex. First the 'grasping' phase, followed by the holding or 'hanging on' phase. One study looking at more than 200 babies found the palmar reflex to be strongest in the first 12 days, and, though less frequent it was always evident up to five months. It is usually inhibited by the time the baby is a year old (Giordano 1953, cited in Goddard Blythe 2009). From an evolutionary perspective, it would seem that this reflex is linked to the primate's need to grasp onto the mother's fur whilst moving. Babies no longer need to do this but as A. Jean Ayres describes:

Evolution occurs very slowly and nature does not readily give up a form of behaviour that has served survival for millions of years. Thus the operations of our nervous system are based upon the needs of the animals from which man evolved, and also the needs of man before he became civilised. These built-in responses provide building blocks for the development of more advanced abilities.

(Ayres 2005:16)

It would seem that our early history as primates is reflected in the fact that the palmar reflex is particularly triggered by contact with hair. Ever had a baby grasp hold of a handful of your hair? Now you know why it can be so difficult to get them to let go again! It seems the grip is stronger before feeding than it is after the child has fed (Goddard Blythe 2009) so it might be even more of a struggle with a hungry baby.

Babkin reflex

Linked to the palmar reflex is the Babkin reflex (not to be confused with the Babinski reflex discussed later in this chapter), which is sometimes called the palmar-mandibular reflex. This is active from birth until around four months and is triggered when quick pressure is applied to the palms of the baby's hands. The reflex response is to bring the head forward and to the midline with the mouth open (Fiorentino 1981, cited in Goddard Blythe 2009) ready to receive the nipple or bottle, which in turn triggers sucking movements when it comes into contact with the mouth. Using the Babkin reflex can help a reluctant baby to begin to feed. Sally Goddard Blythe describes this as an example of a 'hand to mouth sensorimotor link' (Goddard Blythe 2009:107) and draws comparisons with the way hand-reared kittens knead with their claws when sucking from a bottle.

Hand and mouth

The connections between the hands and the mouth have important implications for later speech development. Some children with a history of speech difficulties or language delay also have a problem with fine motor control that suggests the same 'motor centres' of the brain may be involved in both. There may also be an 'overflow of movements from hand to mouth so that the mouth moves when the hands are engaged in a task, or the hands are involuntarily active while speaking' (Goddard Blythe 2009:109). Think of the child (or adult) whose tongue protrudes through the mouth or cheek, when they are writing or using their hands to do something. We think of it as an indicator of concentration during a task that presents some difficulty, but it also reminds us how strong the links between hand and mouth are.

Figure 4.4 Hands and mouth work together in early stages of physical development.

Dropped it!

The palmar reflex should be gradually inhibited by the fifth month when we expect to see babies start to drop things – and to wait for adults to pick them up for them again! This is because the reflex is becoming inhibited and they are able to choose to let go of something, although it happens mostly by accident at first. We tend to attach more importance to being able to hold on to something, but at this stage it is the 'letting go' that indicates physical progress. Without it, many of the later hand and finger skills just wouldn't be possible.

Developing a pincer grip

By nine months, a child will typically be beginning to use a pincer grip with the thumb and index finger and their skill and dexterity will continue to develop. Interestingly, when a child begins to write, they revisit earlier movement patterns and so first grasp a crayon with their whole hand, using gross motor movements to make marks. The table does not support the hand, so the whole arm is used. It usually takes a while before a 'tripod' pincer grip is used. This involves the index finger extending and guiding the pencil, which is supported by the third finger.

Link with laterality

Another important development is that one hand can now do something without the other copying or 'mirroring' the action, which has implications for our abilities to use tools of all sorts. When we cut something out, we hold the paper with one hand and use the scissors in a completely different way with the other. Western eating implements demand a similar differentiation – the hand holding a fork has to work differently from the hand with the knife.

What might happen if the palmar reflex is retained?

A retained palmar reflex can lead to poor manual dexterity.

- Difficulties with pincer grip and rapid finger movements may lead to poor writing grip and problems with the fine muscle skills required for tool use.

- The palm of the hand may continue to be hypersensitive to touch.

- There might continue to be an overflow between hand and mouth movements – the mouth or tongue moves when the hands are doing something or the hands move excessively during speech, as referred to in the rooting reflex.

- Moving the fingers independently (e.g. playing piano/using computer keyboard) weakens other muscles and can cause the child to slouch, leading to back pain.
    (Pound 2013; Goddard Blythe 2009; RNR 2015)

Plantar and Babinski reflexes (push away)

The plantar reflex has similarities with the palmar reflex in that it is also a 'grasping' reflex triggered by touch or pressure, in this case on the sole of the foot, towards the toes, rather than the heel. It results in flexion of the toes and, although not as strong as the grasp in the palmar reflex, it could still allow the toes to clutch at something. It should be inhibited by the time the child is starting to stand, typically around 12 months.

The foot is a busy place for reflexes in the first year of life, because active at the same time is the Babinski reflex (also known as the extensor plantar response), which is also present at birth. It is triggered by stroking the outside of the sole up to the little toe and across to the big toe, making all the toes fan out and the big toe overextend.

The pyramidal tract

It is thought that the presence of this reflex is linked to the maturation of the corticospinal tract. This is also known by its easier name – the pyramidal tract – because of the shape created by the crossover of its very long axons. These originate in the brain at the cerebral cortex and then cross over at the top of the cervical spine before they travel down each side of the spinal cord. These are some of the longest nerves in the body, connecting the brain to the voluntary muscles in the feet. Myelination of these nerves starts at the top (in the head) and works down so that the nerves in the feet are the last to become myelinated; so it takes a while before the baby is able to have full control of the muscles in their feet. The two reflexes are believed to work together, one to build the corticospinal pathways and the other to help inhibit the reaction, with the Babinski reflex gradually giving way to the plantar reflex, which lasts until the child is starting to walk, typically around 12 months of age (Goddard Blythe 2009).

Talking toes!

We tend to notice how babies wave their arms and feet when they are excited, but watch their toes and you will see just how much they flex and extend them whether or not there is any pressure stimulus. Goddard Blythe describes how babies from around 6 months make a game of extending and flexing their toes:

> In effect the toes appear to carry on a 'conversation' at this stage in development, becoming more active when the infant is excited or just before it vocalizes, rather as if the motor pathways are involved in preparing the system for the utterances or babble which precedes intelligible speech. It is probable that continuous exercise of the pathways involved also helps to develop connections within the corticospinal (pyramidal) tract.
>
> (Goddard Blythe 2009:112)

Stretching out a big toe away from the other toes is also useful for helping the baby 'push off' from the ground when they start to crawl.

What might happen if the Babinski and plantar reflexes are retained?

■ Because of the way the reflexes affect the muscles in the feet they can cause problems with gait (the way a person walks) when they are retained.

■ They may be the cause for some (but not all) children who walk on their toes and for those who are very sensitive to uneven surfaces.

■ They may also be indicators of problems with the corticospinal tract as in multiple sclerosis.

■ The Babinski reflex is sometimes temporarily present when blood glucose levels drop to abnormally low levels (hypoglycaemia) but will disappear again shortly after glucose levels have risen.

Spinal galant (squirming)

This reflex exists in the womb and is important in the birth process. Sensitive spots on the back cause the baby to 'squirm' and arch the body one way and then the other as they touch the walls of the womb and birth canal, assisting in delivery. It is believed the spinal galant reflex may also have a link with the creeping and crawling stages of motor development as if 'contributing to the function of a tail' (Goddard Blythe 2009:126). Think of the way a crocodile or lizard swishes its tail from side to side as its body arches sideways as it creeps along. The reflex should be naturally inhibited through opportunities for wriggling and kicking when lying on the back, as well as through baby massage.

What might happen if the spinal galant reflex is retained?

There may continue to be lower back sensitivity if the reflex is retained, which may lead to restlessness and fidgeting, particularly if the sensitive spots come into contact with furniture or clothes. Goddard Blythe describes children with retained spinal galant reflexes as like 'bluebottles in the house' constantly buzzing because if they manage to contain their urge to move, then the energy is usually diverted into making a noise (Goddard Blythe 2009:127)! These children often relax or work better lying on the floor, where the reflex is less likely to be triggered.

Postural reflexes

These enable babies to move from being creatures whose only independent positions are lying on their tummies or backs (prone or supine) to being upright with their heads aligned squarely on their shoulders.

The head-righting reflex is particularly important. A baby's head is the heaviest part of their body and although there is little control over it immediately after birth, within weeks we begin to see increasing control as they start to lift and hold it independently. The head-righting reflexes work with the muscles in the neck, shoulders, back and torso and are very important in enabling the child to maintain control of the head whatever position they are in, whether moving or still.

Working with primitive reflexes to address emotional and cognitive difficulties

'All reflexes presumably have a function at the time in development when they are active. Just as behaviours such as thumb sucking or bed wetting are considered normal at one stage in life but become inappropriate if they persist at a later stage, so primitive reflexes have a positive influence in the first six months of life, but their influence becomes increasingly negative if they remain active beyond the normal period of inhibition.'

(Goddard Blythe 2009:47–48).

It is worth remembering this when we consider how reflexes retained from a much younger stage of development may affect a child's behaviour. The child may look one age on the outside, but their behaviour (or ability level) may be that of a younger child. If the body isn't able to support the child at their age level, then inappropriate behaviour is often not because they *'won't'* do something properly, but because they *can't* do it yet.

The more we understand about the impact of retained reflexes on emotional and cognitive development, the better able we are to find approaches that can address some of the difficulties that can arise. Organisations such as INPP, Rhythmic Movement Training and Neurological Reorganisation have developed therapeutic movement activities that allow the brain to catch up and fill in the gaps in reflex inhibition. These have been very successful in addressing learning and emotional or behavioural challenges in children (and adults) who have been failed by conventional remedial approaches. The difference between these approaches and others that focus just on gross motor movement, is that these therapies go much deeper, revisiting the developmental movement patterns that were missed in early infancy and providing the brain with a 'second chance' to catch up and fill in the gaps. Licensed clinicians trained by these organisations have had some considerable success in addressing a wide range of conditions and disorders including dyslexia, dyspraxia (DCD), Attention Deficit Disorder (ADD), Asperger's Syndrome, anxiety and panic disorders, and reading and writing problems. See the More Information section for further details.

Partnership with parents

Some parents may have learned about primitive reflexes from their midwife or health visitor; others may know very little about them.

- Consider the best ways to share information and raise awareness about primitive reflexes that support your particular community of parents.

- This might be through posters and photographs, directly through information sessions or indirectly during stay and play sessions, baby massage or other parental support groups.

■ Remember that parents may be anxious or unsettled by some of the information, so be sensitive to their concerns and signpost them to further advice and guidance if necessary.

■ Raise awareness of the importance of physical play and movement to help release reflexes.

■ Use information about reflexes to explain why you encourage children to spend time crawling, playing and even working on the floor and outside on the grass etc.

■ Remember, as practitioners, we are not in a position to diagnose particular conditions, but our responsibility is to share our understanding that the best way to support children's health and development is through a wide range of movement play.

Partnership with professionals

Information about primitive reflexes may be new to colleagues working with older children or in other agencies. Consider:

■ What might be the best ways to share this information with them and provide support where needed.

■ What may be available in terms of external training support for you and how you can access this.

■ How you could develop partnerships to support continuing professional development.

Summary

Primitive reflexes play a major role in our survival. They are there at birth and all have important functions. But they need to become inhibited over time so that they don't impact on later development. When they are retained they can cause a range of difficulties and be implicated in many behaviours.

Implications for practice

The more we understand about primitive reflexes, their functions and their impact, the better equipped we are to provide the right kind of environment and experiences to help them become inhibited, so that they don't have a negative effect on future development.

This involves:

■ Being aware of our own physicality and recognising the part that retained reflexes may have had in our own physical development;

- Sensitively raising awareness among parents of the relevance of primitive reflexes, the importance of physical play and the value of opportunities for playful movement to help inhibit them at appropriate stages;

- Recognising the effects that retained reflexes may have on behaviours and development and using this information to better understand children and their next steps for progress.

Please remember that if you have concerns about a child's physical development you should always seek further advice and guidance.

Playful ideas to help inhibit or release primitive reflexes

The following are ideas for movement play that are good for general health and wellbeing and may also help to integrate some early reflexes. Please note: these ideas do not form a programme for reflex integration – they are everyday ideas for movement that children will often initiate themselves or will enjoy joining in with when adults initiate them in playful ways. However, it is useful for us as practitioners to see the link between these playful actions and specific reflexes. Although some ideas may seem age-specific, they can also be adapted to suit children at most stages of development within the EYFS and even beyond. Use them spontaneously, responding 'in the moment' to what your observations tell you about a child's developmental readiness, as well as in short bursts of structured activity in small groups, if and when appropriate.

Moro (startle)

Starfish. Lying on the back, curl up, bringing elbows and knees in close to the body. Sometimes open out slowly; other times fling the arms and legs in and out as quickly as you can.

Hugs, cuddles and gentle holding naturally help to inhibit the Moro reflex. Find lots of reasons to spontaneously hug throughout the day. Invent your own hugging games or incorporate hugging into traditional ones e.g. Hug Tag. The catcher has to hug rather than tag. Once hugged, you must stand still until someone else can free you from your frozen state with another hug.

Startle games, such as Peek-a-Boo, played with fun and sensitivity can help inhibit the Moro reflex, especially if they involve physical sensations and lots of comforting holds and hugs, e.g. Humpty Dumpty, where the child falls through the adult's knees, or Horsey Horsey when they are jogged on the knees and thrown high.

ATNR (fencing)

Snow angels. Lie on your back in the snow and spread out the arms and legs to create 'angel' shapes. Just as much fun to do lying on the grass or in the sand!

Pencil rolls. Lie straight with the hands by the sides and roll from side to side or over and over.

Crocodile crawl. Play crocodiles and alligators and crawl around on the belly. Attach a tail and swish it as you go. Make the most of the interest in reptiles and find stories and non-fiction books about them. Go pond dipping and look out for newts, to add to experience.

Snakes and slugs. Add other creatures that move on their tummies.

STNR (rocking)

Row, row, row your boat. A classic game enjoyed by children of all ages.

Rock, tip and tilt. Try finding other ways for rocking, tipping and tilting. Gym balls are good for this activity.

From hand to hand. Anything that involves both hands working separately but in co-operation is good for this reflex and also for the TLR (aligning), e.g. passing a stick around the back or tossing a ball from hand to hand.

Babinski (push away)

Foot massage. A lovely activity for soothing and calming.

Go barefoot. Although safety will obviously be an issue, do make the most of opportunities for children (and adults) to leave off their shoes and socks and experience a range of different surfaces, e.g. grass, stone etc. Provide a range of different textures taped to the floor for indoor barefoot games, e.g. bubble wrap, fur fabric etc.

Pick up toes. See what you can pick up with your toes – try screwed up paper, beanbags and pom-poms as well as objects of different size and texture.

Palmar reflex (grasp)

Hand printing. Encourages stretching and flattening the hand.

Scrunching and crumpling. Use paper, fabric, etc. for scrunchy fun. Then smooth and flatten it out again using the flat of the hand. Older children might enjoy drawing/colouring the resulting patterns and shapes.

Let rip. Tearing up paper into strips is a valuable activity for the hands. Make the most of scrap paper and involve the children in ripping it up before it goes to the recycling.

Monkey bars and ladders and any activity that involves grasping and letting go helps inhibit hand reflexes.

Finger games and songs. Make up your own to add to the traditional repertoire.

Spinal galant (squirming)

Do the Twist. Find some lively music and enjoy twisting your feet, knees, hips and body.

Bum shuffle. With legs out straight, try shuffling backwards and forwards across the whole floor.

Some of the above ideas are adapted from Dempsey (2013).

5 | Sensory processing and integration

This chapter considers the importance of sensory development and introduces the vestibular and proprioceptive senses. We consider the difficulties some children have in integrating sensory experience and why it matters to their all round development.

Sense and sensibility

HAVE A THINK ABOUT... AN EARLY POSITIVE 'SENSORY MEMORY'

It might be...

- A sight, a sound or a smell

- Being cuddled, tickled, stroked

- It could be a sensation – the feel of something against your skin or a movement

- Rocking, swaying, swinging, rolling, bouncing

- Being thrown up in the air

- Running, jumping, sliding, climbing

- Getting messy.

Some people find it easy to summon up memories like this, for others it is much harder. Do this activity in a group and you will usually find that once people begin talking about these kinds of memories, it will trigger something for everybody. Remember the purpose of this task is to relate to POSITIVE sensory experience. Just take some time to wallow in the lovely physical memories.

Now think about...

- How rich is the sensory environment you provide for the children you work with?

- Are there areas of sensory stimulation that receive a lot of attention – e.g. visual?

- What areas would benefit from more attention?

How many senses?

The usual answer to this question is 'five' – sight, hearing, smell, taste and touch. But these are just the 'external' senses that pick up information from our environment and from everything going on around us. Specialists in child development now tend to agree that there are at least two more 'internal' senses that are vitally important to our functioning. These are the vestibular and proprioceptive senses, though it might be simpler to think of them as the sense of movement and the sense of internal body awareness. These two senses are so important that the whole next chapter will be devoted to them.

All our senses do more than simply pick up information like 'receivers' to our brains – they also guide and influence our reactions to what they are telling us (Nurse 2009:33). They are 'the filters through which we internalise the world around us and come to know our own bodies' (Connell and McCarthy 2014:51). As such, it is perceptions and feelings that we are often referring to when we talk about the senses and the physical 'sensations' that accompany them (Durie 2005, cited in Pound 2013:27). Even more crucially, they all provide the neural activity that actually develops and builds our brains and nerve networks in the first place.

Making connections

Learning seems to be all about making connections and this is actually what is happening in our brains when our senses are stimulated. As described in Chapter 1, electrical activity across the synapses (gaps) between a neuron and an axon makes a connection between the two and each time the same information is filtered through the senses to the brain, the connection is quicker and the neural pathway becomes stronger. These pathways are reinforced so that the sensory messages are filtered much more quickly each time, and what was once new information becomes something usual and 'understood'. You probably can't remember the first time you tasted ice cream, but it was probably a very novel experience. Babies and young children are generally accustomed to creamy food and drinks, but the combination of creaminess and iciness is likely to come as a sensory surprise to the mouth, although sight and possibly smell may be the first senses to be triggered by ice cream, with taste soon to follow. Once we have tasted ice cream many times, we are not only accustomed to the taste, smell and feel of it, but our brains can now also *imagine* what it feels like to eat ice cream. The connections in our brain are now so strong that we will come to associate just the words themselves (in whatever languages we learn them) with the taste and tactile experience of eating ice cream.

Prior experience

Because we can now anticipate the experience, we can also now make decisions as to whether or not we want to repeat it, so the senses play another important role in helping us work out how we feel about all these sensations we are experiencing. Do we like them or do we not? Do they make us feel good or do they make us feel bad? Do they irritate or soothe us? Do they hurt us or make us feel better? Do they stimulate us in a good way or a bad way? Do we want more of the sensation or less? Will we seek the sensation out, or try to avoid it? Do we like this ice cream stuff and want more of it, or will we shake our heads when offered it? Not only are we making connections with the sensations ice cream provides us with, but we are also making emotional and cognitive connections with our prior experience of it, in order to be able to make choices about eating it in the future.

'Filing' sensory experience

As Connell and McCarthy suggest, the child's brain starts 'by *associating* the new with what he already knows, which enables him to make initial assumptions' (Connell and McCarthy 2014:52). It as though the brain has filing cabinets filled with prior experience for us to search through and draw on, though in this technological age perhaps the computer analogy of a 'drop-down list' might work better, especially as the process needs to be a lot faster than rifling through a drawer full of files (O'Connor 2015). When a new experience is meaningful, we have some prior experience with which to connect it. This helps us make sense of it initially, then helps us to remember it and to be able to draw on the information again quickly if we need it again.

Use it or lose it

The more an experience is repeated, the further up the 'list' it goes, and so we can find it more easily! A completely new sensation might be 'filed', but if we have no further experiences that encourage us to refer back to it again and again, then it is likely to be forgotten. This fits with what we know about children's brain development. A new baby's brain contains billions of neurons at birth. Lots of new connections are being made constantly, but many neurons will be 'pruned' away if they're not needed. This is reasonable in that there is only so much information that is useful (a drop-down list that is too long isn't very helpful), but it also emphasises the importance of repetition and connected experiences in shaping the brain. 'Use it or lose it' makes very good sense here, as most of us who use computers will have learned!

The learning process

This also links with what we know about learning and cognitive development. It is easier to learn something when we have some background knowledge or experience than learning something from scratch. If it is harder to find connections with what you already know then it is harder for the new information to 'stick'. However, if you have a good grounding in the subject, you have plenty of material on which to hang new and unfamiliar information. And if you are starting a subject from scratch (e.g. learning a language or a practical skill) the information sticks more quickly and reliably if you repeat the learning soon after and frequently. More connections can then be made and the learning (and understanding) process continues. If babies and young children are acquiring lots of new and important information through their senses, then they need the chance to make lots of connections with the familiar, as well as the stimulation of new experiences.

Judgement and response

So to go back to our ice cream analogy, what happens when a child has experienced this cold, white, creamy stuff and they know they like it, but then they are offered something else the grown-ups call ice cream – but it's brown? Only when the child has tasted it will they be able to make the *judgement* that chocolate ice cream is as nice as vanilla! Or maybe not, because judgement leads to a *response* – they either like it or they don't – and, as familiarity with children teaches us, 'anything new can spark a highly charged response. Whatever his reaction, he'll be a little wiser for the experience and a little more prepared for the next new thing' (Connell and McCarthy 2014:53). Now chocolate ice cream has been added to the child's 'drop-down list' of ice creams, and will in time be added to more categories such as 'treats', 'puddings', and 'foods that live in the freezer', as well as 'things you can eat in the park' or that you can 'buy from a van' (O'Connor 2015)! This is an example of what is described by Connell and McCarthy (2014:65) as the four levels of sensory learning:

- Recognition
- Association
- Judgement
- Response.

HAVE A THINK ABOUT... SENSORY LEARNING AS AN ADULT

When were you last surprised by something you had never seen, smelled, touched, heard or tasted before?

Is it possible as an adult to still find an entirely new sensory experience? Let's hope so!

Can you remember what it felt like as a child to be experiencing a new sensation?

How often do you see, and observe closely, the children you work with experiencing the four levels of sensory learning?

How far do you let children explore new sensations or sensory experiences in their own way?

Are you a good 'sensory role model'? Are you always on the lookout for possible new sensory experiences for yourself as well as for the children with whom you work?

Movement and the senses

Physical movement is crucial to sensory development. Just think for a moment about a range of external sensory experiences and how movement might be involved. Seeing, smelling, tasting, feeling and touching all involve movement of and within the body to a greater or lesser extent. Even hearing involves tiny movements of bones and hair inside the ear as the sound waves reach them. Let's look at another example of eating as a sensory experience, but with something a little healthier than ice cream this time.

- Eating and tasting a piece of fruit such as a strawberry involves movement of the mouth, lips, tongue, jaw and muscles in the face, as well as possibly the fingers, hand, arm and upper body as you hold and feel it.

- Smelling a strawberry involves reaching or bringing the nose close to it. Hairs inside the nose move, as do the chest and abdomen as you breathe in to smell the aroma.

- Looking at a strawberry involves movement of the muscles in the eye as well as the head, neck and other parts of the body as you turn or bend to look at it.

- Hearing the sounds made as you suck or chew on the strawberry, or squish it in your fingers, involves movements in your ears.

'Move-to-learn' cycle

But this link between movement and the senses is a reciprocal one – physical movements also stimulate the senses, which then 'act as the fuel that keeps the child's move-to-learn cycle moving' (Connell and McCarthy 2014:51). To continue with our example of eating as a sensory experience, a young child's very first taste of an ice cream (or strawberry) will probably trigger not just movement in the mouth, lips, tongue, jaw etc. but also in their arms, hands and fingers as they reach out to feel it, or in their head and neck as they clamp their mouth shut and shake their head to resist it. If they like the tasting experience, they might attempt to stick their fingers in (the ice cream) or maybe try to grab the fruit or the spoon/cone to make sure they get more! The movements ensure more stimulation, bringing more information to the brain.

A multi-sensory life

HAVE A THINK ABOUT... WALKING IN THE PARK ON A SUMMER'S DAY

What can your eyes see? Trees? Grass? People?

What can your ears hear? Birdsong? Children playing?

What can your nose smell? Grass? Flowers? Barbeques?

What can your skin feel? A breeze? Sunshine?

As well as all the above, your vestibular and proprioceptive senses will be busy as you negotiate your way through the park, walking, running, kicking a ball, riding on the swings or sliding down the slide. Your sense of taste may even be active if you stop for a drink, an ice cream or a picnic on the grass. Life really is a 'multi sensory event' (Biel and Peske 2009:28).

'Foregrounding' sensory input

How do we manage all these sensations at once and are we conscious of them all at the same time? Although we may be conscious of some more than others, we can choose to 'foreground' some of them more. Perhaps it's the taste of your sandwich, or the sensation of coming down the slide that comes to the fore, so that you become less conscious for a moment of the birds singing? This ability to foreground is very important as it allows us to select and prioritise sensory input from the constant bombardment of stimuli provided by our environment. Difficulties with foregrounding sensory input can make it very difficult to concentrate and focus on a task or objective. In her book *Sensory Integration and the Child: Understanding Hidden Sensory Challenges*, A. Jean Ayres suggests an exercise to help us appreciate what it might feel like to have difficulty foregrounding the appropriate sensory information for a task. Imagine you have gone into an unfamiliar warehouse to find a box, in amongst lots of other boxes. You will probably need to foreground information from your visual sense in particular, to help you find what you are looking for. But then the lights go out, so you can't see anymore, but still you need to search for this box. You search on, perhaps relying more on touch and sense of body position than you were before, in order to find your way around. Then the fire alarm goes off and the sprinklers come on, making it really hard to concentrate on your search and to shut out the noise from the alarm and the feeling of being soaked by the sprinklers. How likely is it that you might now just give up and go home without the box (Ayres 2005:10)?

HAVE A THINK ABOUT... SENSORY FOREGROUNDING

You are on a very long train journey and have with you a book /newspaper/magazine, that you are looking forward to reading.

But…

The train carriage and the space around you is very dirty (visual/sight).

The fabric on your seat has a very rough texture (tactile/touch).

You are right by a very smelly toilet (olfactory/smell).

There is a screaming child across from you and a person with 'leaking' headphones playing loud music sat next to you (aural/sound).

Which of the above will you notice most?

Which will absolutely prevent you from being able to focus on your reading?

Which of them could you block out easily so that you can still 'foreground' your ability to read?

Some people are very good at blocking out sensory experiences in order to concentrate, but most people will have at least one 'sense' that is more prominent and foregrounded under stress, so that you can't block it out and focus on something else. Being able to continue reading through all the above suggests very good sensory integration – or a very good book!

Sensory processing and sensory integration

For sensory input to be useful, it has to flow quickly and without interruption to exactly the right parts of the brain in order to be processed effectively. Problems with sensory processing have long been recognised as symptoms of medical conditions such as multiple sclerosis, vertigo and stroke (Biel and Peske 2009:13), but more recently we have seen a raised awareness of the potential cognitive and emotional problems of poor sensory processing and integration of the senses. The two terms 'sensory processing' and 'sensory integration' are often used in the same context and Sensory Processing Disorder (SPD) is an umbrella term to cover a range of difficulties with sensory processing and integration.

Jigsaw puzzle

What do we mean by sensory integration? Connell and McCarthy describe it as a 'jigsaw puzzle' with all the different sensory experiences making up the pieces. Each one needs to be integrated and in exactly the right place before the child can see the full picture and is able to 'make sense' of all the information provided by the sensory experience.

'Until the brain integrates all the pieces, the child may not fully understand the picture. Sensory integration, therefore, greatly affects not only what a child perceives but also how he interprets, understands and responds to sensory information – in other words, how he learns' (Connell and McCarthy 2014:53).

Sensory impairment and sensory processing

It is important to note here that having a problem with sensory processing or sensory integration is not the same as having a sensory impairment. For a child with a hearing impairment, for example, sounds may be dulled, distorted or totally absent due to a malfunction in the mechanisms of the ear or hearing system. However, a child with an audio processing difficulty may have perfect hearing but the difficulties lie with the brain's ability to process, modulate or discriminate sound in ways that make it possible – and tolerable – for the child to make all the right connections between a whole range of sounds (including words) and their meanings (O'Connor 2015).

Difficulties with sensory integration

As A. Jean Ayres wrote:

> Sensory integration is not an either/or matter. We don't have perfect sensory integration or none at all. None of us organizes sensations perfectly. Happy, productive, well-co-ordinated people may come the closest to perfect sensory integration. Some people have especially good sensory integration, others just average and others, poor.
>
> (Ayres 2005:8)

Red flags

A study published in 2009 suggested that as many as 1 in 6 children may have difficulties with sensory processing (Ben-Sasson et al. 2009), while an earlier study found the figure to be 1 in 20 (Ahn et al. 2004). The studies considered a child to have difficulties if the range of sensory symptoms experienced were significant enough to affect aspects of their everyday lives and functioning. The website for the Sensory Processing Disorder (SPD) Foundation (USA) provides a list of symptoms, referring to them as 'Red Flags' that may alert parents, practitioners and clinicians to problems with sensory processing. For infants, toddlers and pre-schoolers these include:

- Problems with eating or sleeping
- Irritability when being dressed; uncomfortable in clothes
- Rarely plays with toys
- Resists cuddling, arches away when held
- Cannot calm self
- Floppy or stiff body, motor delays
- Over-sensitive to touch, noises, smells, other people
- Difficulty making friends
- Difficulty dressing, eating, sleeping, and/or toilet training
- Clumsy; poor motor skills; weak
- In constant motion; in everyone else's face and space
- Frequent or long temper tantrums.

(SPD Foundation 2015)

Risk factors

The SPD Foundation also suggests that many of the risk factors for sensory processing difficulties seem to relate to prenatal and delivery experiences, including:

- Low birth weight
- Prematurity
- Prenatal complications
- Maternal stress
- Maternal illness
- Maternal use of medications

- Delivery complications
- Assisted delivery methods.

(SPD Foundation 2015)

SPD and other conditions

However, this does not mean that the existence of any of the above factors will automatically lead to difficulties with sensory processing. Similarly, some children with SPD have other medical or learning issues, including ADHD and autistic spectrum disorders, though the existence of SPD in a child does NOT automatically mean that they will have other issues or are on the autistic spectrum. Some children with poor sensory processing may have very typical development in all other ways and be of average or above average intelligence. Adoptive parents and foster carers often find that children who have experienced early trauma and poor attachments have some degree of sensory processing disorder, particularly when their early lives have been marked by a lack of loving and affectionate touch together with unhealthy levels of over or under stimulation. The approach needed to support and treat a child who is touch sensitive because of abuse or neglect may have to be very different to that required for a child from a secure background who has SPD (Radwan 2009).

'Traffic jams in the brain'

A. Jean Ayres was at the forefront of developing the theory of sensory integration, and her approach was based on the pioneering work of Florence Scott. Ayres was very clear that every child with poor sensory integration might show a different set of symptoms, but her explanation of what she believed was going on in the brain was quite straightforward. She likened it to a 'traffic jam in the brain' (Ayres 2005:47) where the messages from sensory stimulation are prevented from getting to where they need to be in the brain for the child to be able to make sense of them.

Responding to sensory processing difficulties

Unfortunately, a lot of the symptoms for SPD mentioned above are often misunderstood, and judged instead, as undesirable or inappropriate behaviour that children (or parents) need to bring under control. This is unfair but as Ayres points out:

> it is easy to recognise unpleasant behaviour, but more difficult to recognise the neurological influences that underlie that behaviour. When a child behaves poorly, it is important to realise that a great deal of that behaviour may come from ordinary sensations that this child cannot integrate. If he cannot organise sensations, he cannot organise his behaviour.

(Ayres 2005:155)

Tactile sensitivity

Some children experience a heightened sensitivity to touch sensations. This can be displayed as either under or over-responsiveness to tactile experiences. Where there is an under responsiveness, the child is likely to constantly seek out tactile stimulation in order to feel something, demanding (and giving) lots of physical contact and not always being able to self-regulate tactile experiences. Some children are much less comfortable with tactile experiences, due to their heightened sensitivity. So what feels like a gentle touch or stroke to one child can be unbearably unpleasant to the child with tactile defensiveness. Most of us will jump or react to unpleasant or uninvited touch sensations like an insect crawling on the skin or being touched when we weren't expecting it. But these children experience many more tactile sensations as unpleasant and offensive, including sometimes the feeling of clothes or labels touching the skin, or mud and dirt on the hands or face. As discussed earlier in this chapter, most of us can manage to inhibit sensations that we are feeling constantly and only bring them to our attention if we choose to. The child with tactile defensiveness is not able to do that and the experience can be excruciating and intolerable, leading to what might be described as over-reactive behaviour, but perfectly understandable in the child's circumstances. These children may not like to be touched and don't always enjoy cuddles and hugs even from people they know well. This can interfere with social relationships and even playing with other children can become fraught with anxiety and distress, particularly if the child reacts with aggression or withdraws from others.

'The child with tactile defensiveness is in quite a quandary; he needs more touch than other children, but he is less able to modulate tactile impulses and use them to keep his nervous system balanced' (Ayres 2005:106).

HAVE A THINK ABOUT... WHAT TACTILE DEFENSIVENESS MIGHT FEEL LIKE

You are walking down a dark alleyway and think you hear someone or something coming behind you. Then you feel something brushing lightly against your neck.

How easy do you think it would be to tell if it was just a branch of a tree… or something more menacing? How likely are you to react in a calm, relaxed manner? Or are you more likely to react quickly and negatively to the experience? Given that the above touch sensation would be less threatening and possibly welcomed in other circumstances, what is it that heightens your reaction in this case? Can you think of children you know (or have known) who react in this way to tactile experience? How might you change your responses to them as a result of becoming more aware of the impact of tactile defensiveness?

Impact on learning and behaviour

Think for a moment about how it feels to wear an unbearably scratchy jumper, or to be covered in itchy insect bites. Or perhaps you got very wet in the rain and have to sit in your wet clothes rather than change them. Now imagine yourself in an important meeting, or listening to a complicated lecture or looking after a fractious baby whilst dealing with any of the above. How well are you able to concentrate on the data presented in the meeting, or the complex information of the lecture – and how easy is it to be patient and responsive to the baby and not begin to feel fractious yourself?

In just the same way, the child with heightened tactile sensitivity may struggle to concentrate on what you are telling them, to listen attentively to the story you are reading or be patient with other children when having to wait in line for their dinner. There is no point telling a child with tactile defensiveness that they don't need to overreact, or to punish them for bad behaviour or for making 'poor choices' when they are feeling so intensely uncomfortable most of the time. The child's discomfort is real and to deny it will only add to their negative feelings about themselves. (The above examples are adapted from Ayres 2005.)

Providing a bridge

Inevitably some children will find ways to avoid experiences they don't enjoy and will miss out on the very experiences their brains need in order to create the neural pathways that will modulate the sensitivity. Although we can provide a stimulating and supportive environment, it is particularly important that the drive for tactile experience comes from the children themselves. Our brains interpret differently the touch sensations initiated by ourselves and those we receive from others. For example it is quite hard to tickle yourself, so a child who hates being tickled might be able to tolerate stroking themselves with a feather much better than if someone else were to do it. Providing the opportunity for playful and exploratory activities over which the child has a greater degree of control is reassuring and allows the child to build up new sensory experiences that can help reduce sensitivity. Attuned adults who know their children well will be able to meet the child 'where they are at' and gently provide a bridge to experiences that the child can handle at their own pace.

Ideas for supporting children with tactile defensiveness

- Always reassure children it is all right to just observe other children engaging in an activity and to join in only when they feel ready.

- Help them to feel in control and to know they can stop the activity as soon as they want.

- Provide soft, fleecy blankets and big cushions for wrapping up and for making 'kid sandwiches'. Sleeping bags and lycra 'tubes' are also good for providing gentle tactile pressure.

- Remember that firm and constant pressure is probably less irritating than light ticklish touch; consider using the whole hand rather than just finger tips to touch the child.

- Standing in the middle of a line is a lot harder than standing at the front or the back; this might help reduce agitated behaviour when others brush past them.

- Demonstrate and use new tactile experiences on yourself first. Play with brushes, sponges, lotion, bury hands in sand etc.

Making a mess and building a brain

Messy activities are an important sensory experience for all children.

Messy play involves full sensori-motor experiences. That means it engages the senses, as well as movement. Traditionally, 'messy' activities involve substances like sand and water, paint, glue, dough, chalk, and 'gloopy' stuff like shaving foam, flour and water and soap flakes. These require a certain amount of pre-planning and resourcing, but children are also pretty good at finding their own 'messy' stuff to engage with, particularly dirty puddles and muddy patches!

Although children can usually see and enjoy looking at the messy stuff they are playing with, it is touch that is probably the key sense to be triggered as children poke their fingers into gloopy stuff, or cover their hands (and other body parts) in paint or mud. But smell is also often involved, as well as hearing – just think about all those lovely squelching sounds! When the messy stuff is food-based then taste can also be involved, although, let's face it, we probably all had a sneaky lick of something messy as children, only to discover it didn't taste as nice as it probably looked. Some settings prefer not to use food as a messy activity in order to acknowledge that when there are still many people starving in the world, food should be regarded as a precious commodity and not something to be wasted purely for play. This does not preclude children being able to 'play' with their own food, however, which is an important stage in learning to feed oneself, as well as a vital sensory experience as children learn about food texture and consistency.

Messy play is important because it provides such valuable opportunities for building connections in the brain, helping the child to make sense of repeated experiences and informing their understanding of the world around them. It is also important in the way that it challenges young brains, by being confusing – a concept that Piaget referred to as 'cognitive disequilibrium'. A lump of mud might look solid until you poke your finger in it and discover that it is squishy. As well as learning that we can't always rely on one sense (in this case our eyes) to correctly inform us about the nature of things, it also causes a degree of confusion in the brain. Bernadette Duffy describes how this confusion is important in building creativity as 'the creative process is characterised by risk taking, trying things out and experimenting, and an insight often occurs at the very moment we are confused and have to look deeper' (Duffy 2004).

The outdoors is a great place for messy play. Not only does it reduce some of the anxieties about mess and cleaning up, but it also provides more opportunities for spontaneous messy play that doesn't have to be set up or led by an adult. The weather is often helpful, not just in providing the puddles and mud, but also in washing away the after effects. Ideally every setting should have access to a regular supply of water outside, however, as it is important to involve children in the cleaning up of equipment and the outdoor area in general. Washing and cleaning is just as much of a sensory experience as getting messy in the first place!

HAVE A THINK ABOUT... GETTING MESSY

Do you have children who love messy play?

Are there some you have noticed who prefer not to join in with messy activities?

Why do you think this might be?

Do you have parents who are not keen on messy play?

How can you support them to appreciate the importance of this kind of experience for their children's learning and development?

Messy activities may be a cause of anxiety for some children with tactile defensiveness and they may choose to resist them. Try these ideas to reduce their anxiety:

- Allow children to wear gloves if appropriate.
- Let them put their hand on your hand as you touch something they find unpleasant or stressful.
- Provide tools to use rather than their fingers.
- Offer a doll to use as a substitute for their own bodies, for face painting, playing in mud etc.
- Warming up paint, dough, mud etc. with warm water can make the experience more pleasurable and less threatening.
- Make sure children always have the opportunity to protect their clothes, particularly those children who are anxious about their parents' reactions to paint, mud, dirt etc.

(Ideas adapted from O'Connor 2010)

Adult issues around messy play

As adults, we may have our own sensory issues around dirt and messy play. Inevitably this can sometimes lead to a reluctance to make these kinds of activity and experience available, particularly if we are anxious about clearing up afterwards. Make the most of the outdoors, where the weather usually helps wash the mess away, and choose one or two activities that you find least threatening at first, to build up your confidence. Supportive colleagues can help by sharing out messy activities so that you don't feel overwhelmed. Give yourself time to relax and to play with messy materials by yourself as well as alongside the children.

Partnership with parents

- Some parents may be struggling with behaviours in a child when they know something is not right but have had difficulty getting medical and other professionals to listen to them.

- Take their concerns seriously and find out what is available locally so that you can signpost them to agencies and support groups as well as health and educational professionals who can help them.

- Consider whether attitudes and requirements for clothes/uniforms etc. interfere with children's ability to fully experience movement and multi-sensory play.

- Some parents may need help appreciating the value of play experiences that support sensory development, processing and integration. Provide them with appropriate information and use posters, photos and video clips to explain the four levels of sensory learning and ways they can provide similar experiences at home.

Partnership with professionals

- Help colleagues to look more closely at behaviours causing concern to check for underlying sensory processing issues.

- Find out what advice and information is available locally and nationally from other agencies and websites etc. to support your knowledge and understanding of sensory processing and disorders relating to it.

Summary

This chapter explores the role of five of the main senses in children's physical development and the difficulties some children may experience in processing and integrating the messages sent to the brain by sensory stimulation. It considers the importance of a multi-sensory environment to foster children's individual wellbeing, supporting 'embodied learning'.

Implications for practice

Increasing our awareness of the importance of sensory integration and the implications of sensory processing difficulties prompts us to:

■ Consider the sensory aspects of the environments we create and how suitable they are for children at differing ages and stages of development.

■ Be aware that behaviours we may find challenging could stem from some children's difficulties with sensory processing and that careful responses will be required from us in order to support and assist children's development appropriately.

■ Seek advice and guidance if we are concerned about children's sensory development and processing.

■ Connect with our own sensory experiences, delighting in the positive and seeking to understand those that we find more challenging, so that we can be good 'sensory' role models for the children we work with.

Playful ideas: for supporting sensory processing and integration

As practitioners, it is not our job to diagnose specific conditions or disorders, and it is imperative that we should always seek advice and guidance if we are concerned about a child's development. However, we do have a professional responsibility to remember that children are constantly communicating to us through their behaviour – and that a wider knowledge of sensory processing enables us to better understand what might be going on for some children in their bodies and their brains. Furthermore, the environment we provide (the space, resources and the people) can do a lot to address sensory deficiencies and support natural integration. Although some ideas may seem age-specific, they can also be adapted to suit children at most stages of development within the EYFS and even beyond. Use them spontaneously, responding 'in the moment' to what your observations tell you about a child's developmental readiness, as well as in short bursts of structured activity in small groups, if and when appropriate.

Massage ideas

If you work with babies and haven't already trained in baby massage it is well worth finding out more about it. (See More Information section.) In the meantime, make the most of personal care routines (e.g. nappy changing) for affectionate strokes and cuddles. Clockwise circles on the tummy can be very soothing and help digestion. Gentle rubs or strokes on the back are comforting and can help calm or soothe an agitated or restless baby or older child.

Children of all ages enjoy hand (and feet) massages, with soapy suds or hand lotion. (Check for skin allergies first.)

Try full body swooshes with see-through light fabric (e.g. net or voile). With the child sitting or lying on the floor on their back, drape them with the fabric, keeping eye contact and pull the fabric the length of the body. Vary the speed to add to the drama!

Take a big koosh ball or a soft beach ball and gently roll on different parts of the body.

Movements

Body percussion – Try alone or to a piece of music. Where on your body can you feel the rhythm? Tapping on tummies, backs, heads, shoulders etc. Clapping along, head bobbing, body swaying, feet swooshing.

Floor percussion with hands and feet – Trying out different rhythms and playing along to different tunes

'Raindrop' drumming fingers all over the body can be invigorating. Be firm rather than too gentle.

Floor gym – Sometimes floor space is all that is needed to allow babies safe movement and time to explore what their bodies can do. Make sure the floor is clean and safe, ideally not too soft or too hard. Sit back and watch, providing verbal responses or encouragement and touch when needed.

Resources

Play dough is very good for 'heavy work' of kneading and rolling as well as for sticking fingers into and squishing.

Look out for old Rubik's cubes and other interesting items for fidgety fingers to fiddle with.

Keep a selection of nice scented soaps (floral, fruity, fresh) in a bag to enjoy the smells.

Wrap up in large squares of lycra and push and stretch against the fabric. Make shapes that can be seen from the outside, small or tall, or keep exploring. Lycra 'tubes' (or 'Body Socks') are great for this, as well as for full body wriggles through from top to bottom, like taking a huge jumper off!

Collect different carpet squares (short, shag pile, sheepskin, velour etc.) and enjoy feeling them with bare feet and hands. You can place them where children need them, e.g. under the table or next to them as they listen to a story.

Use straws for gentle blowing and 'doodling' patterns on the skin. Try with feathers too for stroking on bare skin and gently on faces. Encourage children who find 'tickling' sensations a challenge to blow or use the feathers on themselves.

Sucking smoothies or drinking yoghurt through a straw is good exercise for children who have weak mouth muscles or problems with dribbling.

Several suppliers now make 'chewy' jewellery for children who need to chew on things. (See the More Information section.)

6 Looking more closely at vestibular and pro-prioceptive development

This chapter focuses very specifically on the development of the proprioceptive and vestibular systems and considers why they are so fundamental to good physical development.

Being balanced

Vestibular system

Let's begin with the vestibular system and consider why it is so important to our physical, emotional, social and intellectual development.

Goddard Blythe (2004:11) describes balance as 'the Primary Sense' and the oldest of our sensory systems. In technical terms, we use the word vestibular to describe the balance system, which is believed to have evolved first, long before our other senses, though we are not really conscious of it in the way we are with our other senses of sight, smell, hearing etc. This is because when it is working well, it doesn't have a sensation to accompany it and we only know of it through our other sensory systems. These can be good sensations such as the rush of adrenaline when coming down the slide or riding on a roller coaster, or the less happy sensations of motion or sea sickness when the relationship of balance, body and vision is upset (Goddard Blythe 2004:12) or 'out of sync'.

This important sense isn't very well developed at birth but we have a biological drive to move in ways that are essential to stimulate its development.

HAVE A THINK ABOUT... GETTING DIZZY

Are you one of those people who love roller coasters?

Or are you someone who feels sick on a swing?

Were you always the same or have you noticed a change in your attitude to these kinds of activities as you have grown older?

Do you notice children choosing to spin and roll, hang upside down and generally make themselves dizzy?

Are there children who prefer to stay away from those kinds of activities and some who seek out the dizziest of activities on a regular basis?

Feeling dizzy

Children typically like to do all the activities described above, because for them it mostly feels good. When something feels good for a child, they are motivated to do it over and over again and, as we have explored several times already, the repetition of self-initiated activity builds strong neural pathways in the brain and, in this case, develops the vestibular sensory system, which wouldn't develop without the movement to stimulate it. Children instinctively know this and will independently seek out vestibular stimulation in multiple ways through everyday activities. Being in charge of their own vestibular stimulation is important as it means an activity is perfectly tuned to their individual stage of development. In most cases, they know when to stop because they have had enough. We will return later in this chapter to consider the children who have difficulty regulating activity, with either too much or too little sensory seeking.

Figure 6.1 Orla and her mum enjoy playful vestibular activity.

The perfect activities for stimulating the vestibular system are hanging upside down, and spinning and rolling. Doing these activities slowly is particularly important as it helps the brain to absorb and assimilate the lovely physical sensation, although the adrenaline rush of going fast can also feel good too! As Connell and McCarthy suggest, a child needs to be able to go at both speeds to be able to moderate and control their physical activity safely (Connell and McCarthy 2014:88).

Is it me that is moving?

Our vestibular sense is very important for helping us know and understand our physical position in space. We need to know the answers to questions such as 'Is it me moving?' and 'Am I upside down?' and to know when we are still but what we are looking at is moving or upside down. And when we are moving, we need our vestibular system to work in conjunction with the muscles in our eyes, our necks and heads to keep our vision stable so that we can see where we are going and feel a sense of gravitational security. This is why our vestibular sense is so important in guiding us through the process of becoming a 'terranaut' (Barsch 1968) and learning to manage the effects of gravity. Unless we are astronauts, the likelihood is that we will experience gravity throughout our lives and, as we take it for granted, we actually don't notice it.

How does the vestibular system work?

First of all, let's identify the different parts of the vestibular system. It's composed of vestibular receptors in the inner ear and linked to the mid-region of the brain. Because our world is three-dimensional, there are three semicircular canals inside the inner ear. They each contain tiny hairs with nerve endings (cilia), which move about in the fluid surrounding them, in response to the body's movements. The movement of the fluid stimulates the nerve endings, and they send messages to the brain with regard to exactly what the body needs to do to find its balance. If you spin yourself round and round (and you don't have the 'spotting skill' that enables dancers and others to reduce the effects), you will feel dizzy when you stop, because the fluid in the ears will probably continue moving for a short while afterwards. When the fluid stops moving, you will regain your balance and stop feeling dizzy (Connell and McCarthy 2014:85).

Movement is the key

Our vestibular system is crucial to our sense of ourselves in space and in relation to everything around us and movement is the key to enabling the vestibular system to develop well enough to make sense of it all.

That's because movement constantly challenges the brain to adjust and record its understanding of what it feels like to be 'in' and 'out' of balance. And only when the brain has that understanding can it adapt to changing circumstances and help keep us from falling over.

(Connell and McCarthy 2014:85)

The vestibular system and emotional wellbeing

It's easy to see why balance and vestibular development are important for the physical aspects of being able to walk upright and not fall down all the time, but they also play a vital role in our emotional wellbeing.

HAVE A THINK ABOUT... THE PHRASE 'WELL-BALANCED'

What do you think of when you hear it?

Make a list of all the words and phrases that come to mind. Here are a few:

- Stable
- Steady
- Level-headed
- Rational
- Reasonable
- Well-thought-out

- Symmetrical
- Sensible
- Mentally functioning well
- Even-tempered
- Well-adjusted
- Emotionally sound

Now consider how you would describe something or someone who was the opposite of 'well-balanced':

- Unbalanced
- Unstable
- Mentally imbalanced
- Maladjusted
- Dysfunctional

- Wobbly
- 'Not all there'
- Irrational
- Unreasonable
- Unsteady

Why do you think we use 'balance' (or the lack of it) to describe a person's mental or emotional condition?

The title of Sally Goddard Blythe's book *The Well Balanced Child: Movement and Early Learning* (2004) draws our attention to the role played by 'balance' in our appreciation of wellbeing. If we look at the words in the two lists above, it is easy to see which we would want for our children! So why is 'balance' so crucial to wellbeing?

Emotions and the central nervous system

We don't tend to think of our emotions (and emotional health) as a function of our central nervous system. However, there is a neurological basis for every time we feel emotions such as fear, anger, sadness, joy and love. The part of the brain that generates emotionally based behaviour is the limbic system and this depends on the vestibular system to help modulate the input from the senses. Also fundamental to our sense of self and wellbeing is the feeling of 'gravitational security', which is the foundation for building all emotional relationships (Ayres 2005:69).

Gravitational security

Think for a moment about the difference between a 'terranaut' and an 'astronaut'. The terranaut is firmly rooted on the ground, feeling the pull of gravity and a sense of security that they are firmly connected to the earth on which they stand and that they won't float off with nothing to 'ground' them. An astronaut, on the other hand floats about weightlessly (as do most things around them), making it difficult to grasp and keep hold of things and keep themselves in one place. People with a poor sense of gravitational security (and associated emotional challenges) can feel like astronauts floating aimlessly in a void. Ayres comments that 'Gravitational security is so vital to emotional health that nature has given us a strong inner drive to explore gravity and master it' (Ayres 2005:69) and suggests that all other relationships may fail to develop well if the child's relationship to the earth is not secure, leaving them 'lost in space' (Ayres 2005:70). It is worth remembering that one of the most instinctive ways to comfort a child is to rock them gently. Knowing more about the importance of the vestibular system helps us to see why we do this – the gentle motion simultaneously soothes and strengthens the vestibular system and, if it is accompanied with loving, affectionate words and touch, it reinforces attachments and feelings of emotional, as well as gravitational, security.

Vestibular system and language

The vestibular system, working closely with our 'auditory' system (hearing), plays a crucial role in the development and processing of language. The two systems are very closely connected because they both originate in the receptors of the ear. As we've mentioned earlier being *able* to hear isn't the same as being able to *process* what we hear. This is linked to comprehension and our ability to *understand* what we are hearing, which we acquire at the same time as we learn to integrate vestibular sensations through our interactions with our environment. Gradually, we develop more sophisticated auditory processing skills that are important for language development.

These include:

- Auditory discrimination – the ability to differentiate sounds;

- Auditory figure/ground disturbance – the ability to discriminate between sounds in the foreground and those in the background.

Not only is vestibular development crucial for effective auditory processing (Kranowitz 2009), but it is also linked to the physical production of language through speech.

> Language and speech are closely related, but they are not the same. Speech is the physical production of sound. Speech skills depend on smoothly functioning muscles in the throat, tongue, lips, and jaw. The vestibular system influences motor control and motor planning that are necessary to use those fine muscles to produce intelligible speech.
>
> (Kranowitz 2009)

Scream if you want to go faster

If you think about the way that children (and adults) tend to yell when they are running around, or scream when they are on a roller coaster, it isn't too difficult to see that vestibular-stimulating movement and vocalisation might be somehow connected. Ayres suggests that a lack of vestibular stimulation might be linked to the speech and language delay seen in some children. 'It is as if the brain needed a certain amount of vestibular input to produce sounds, and the movements of daily life did not supply the amount needed in these children' (Ayres 2005:76). She noted that quiet or non-speaking children make more sounds and vocalise more when provided with activities that involve vestibular input through movement, swinging, jumping etc., and Kranowitz comments that speech and language therapists report remarkable results from providing a swing to play in, during treatment. Similarly, when occupational therapists treat a child for vestibular dysfunction, the child's speech and language skills can improve alongside their balance and movement skills.

Given our concerns that many children are experiencing reduced levels of early movement experience AND the fact that many settings and schools are noticing an increase in delayed speech and language development (and related issues) among young children, it seems worth considering that there might be a link. An obvious response, therefore, would be to ensure as a matter of course that every child benefits from an environment rich in movement opportunities and vestibular-stimulating experiences, and to monitor the resulting impact on children's speech and language development.

Too much or too little

'There are two types of vestibular disorders that commonly interfere with learning and behaviour: the brain either under reacts to vestibular input or it overreacts' (Ayres 2005:73). Ayres likens this to the volume on a radio – either the dial is set too high or it is too low, and it is uncomfortable to listen at either setting.

Not enough

Children with an *under-reactive* vestibular system seem to have difficulty processing enough vestibular sensation, so they don't get the same natural 'nourishment' provided by movement and play experiences as other children, although the drive and instinct for vestibular stimulation might still be there. This is the child who is constantly spinning around, and likes to swing fast or ride on roundabouts for much longer than anyone else, because they just don't feel dizzy enough unless they do (Ayres 2005:74). Therapists working with these children find that they benefit from extra vestibular activity. **However, it is very important to note that excessive and long lasting spinning and swinging can be very dangerous and should always be avoided.** Children may need help with self-regulation during physical activity, as well as a greater degree of understanding of their need for vigorous and constant movement. An environment rich in opportunities for vestibular activity together with supportive adults who understand the child's motivation for movement (and don't misconstrue it as negative and tiresome behaviour) may help address their vestibular-seeking needs.

Knowing left from right

HAVE A THINK ABOUT... KNOWING YOUR LEFT FROM YOUR RIGHT

Do you know instinctively which is right and which is left?

Do you find it hard to understand how somebody might not instantly be able to do this most simple of things?

Or do you have to stop and think first before being able to know for certain which is which?

Perhaps you have a little trick to help you, like looking at your hands first?

Maybe sometimes you can do it quickly, but you still have to check to make sure you were correct, or you get confused if you have to look in a mirror, or read who is who from right to left in a photograph?

Although as children we all go through the process of learning our left from right, poor integration of both sides of the body can result in difficulties with this. This can be linked to an under-reactive vestibular system (Ayres 2005:75). Those of us who struggle with this often acquire survival or compensation strategies as we get older (like looking at our hands first) but this means using other parts of our brain to compensate for our poor vestibular functioning – we need to rely on thought processes to do something that everyone else does instinctively. This isn't as efficient as we need it to be and slows us down in new or challenging situations such as following directions or navigating for impatient drivers!

Modulation

This is the capacity the brain has to regulate (by increasing or reducing) our neural activity, so that it integrates well with the other functions of our nervous system. We feel relaxed by the gentle stimulus of a rocking chair and aroused by the stimulation of a fast roller coaster. 'A well-modulated vestibular system is important for keeping us in a calm, alert state. It helps to keep the level of arousal in our brains balanced' (Daly and O'Connor June 2009).

Unfortunately, if the arousal levels are not so well balanced it can affect us in a variety of ways, some of which may be fairly insignificant, but some with far reaching effects on our spatial awareness, learning ability and physical and emotional wellbeing.

Too much

Sometimes when the brain finds it difficult to modulate vestibular stimulation it lets in too much information, leading to an overreaction to movement or change of head position. There are two different types of 'hypersensitivity to vestibular input' (Ayres 2005:79). One is gravitational insecurity mentioned earlier, where discomfort is triggered by the position of the head or body regardless of whether the body is moving or still. The other is intolerance to movement itself.

At its most extreme, gravitational insecurity can be very frightening – and hard to explain as it appears not to be rational. Sufferers fear falling even when falling is unlikely or not particularly hazardous, so walking over uneven ground becomes challenging, as do going up and down stairs or holding their head upside down to do somersaults, or even housework! There is a real issue for children with gravitational security as they attempt to keep themselves feeling safe. As Ayres describes,

> To avoid or reduce the stress, he will try to manipulate his environment and other people. This makes him seem obstinate and uncooperative. As a small child, he learns that big adults will move him about without any respect for his oversensitive vestibular system. He then learns ways to control adults and keep them away. The child does not know which situations will be terrifying and which ones will be alright, so he has to control everything as much as possible. Adults then consider this an undesirable personality trait; they try to be the 'boss' and force the child to stop being manipulative. The child then suffers even greater misery.
>
> (Ayres 2005:81)

The 'respectful' approach promoted by Pikler and Gerber addresses some of this anxiety in the way that it encourages parents and carers not to physically manipulate babies and young children into positions they can't yet attain for themselves. Just as importantly, they advocate respect for the child when engaging in personal care routines etc., so that the child is always informed first about what the adult is about to do with them. 'When you approach your baby with an attitude of respect, you let him know what you intend to do and give him a chance to respond' (Gerber 2009).

HAVE A THINK ABOUT... HOW YOU SHOW RESPECT TO CHILDREN AND THEIR PHYSICALITY

Working with young children in a pressured environment, it can be hard not to 'be the boss' when it comes to making decisions about children and their bodies.

Do you sometimes find yourself taking charge and putting a child's shoes on for them, whisking them off to get changed, picking them up to move them along quickly, or holding their head while you briskly wipe their nose or wash their face?

What do you think about the 'respectful' approach encouraged by Gerber and Pikler and how easy is it to replicate in a busy setting?

What do you think practitioners and parents need that would enable them to adopt a more respectful approach to children's physical agency?

Intolerance to movement

We commonly see intolerance to movement in children who suffer from motion sickness, whether travelling or playing on moving toys or equipment. Sometimes they might even feel uncomfortable watching someone else moving or spinning! This is likely to be because input from the semicircular canals in the ear is not being modulated properly.

Children with vestibular hypersensitivity are less likely to want to engage in vigorous activity that stimulates their vestibular system. However, gentle, supported stimulation with a strong focus on emotional support as well as physical can be beneficial. NEVER force a child to spin or twirl. Gentle rocking or swaying in your arms, on your lap or in a rocking chair may be stimulation enough. Find more ideas to support vestibular development in playful ways at the end of this chapter.

The impact of poor vestibular development

Although unpleasant and inconvenient, motion sickness or not being able to tell left from right may not seem like very serious conditions. But poor vestibular development may be at the root of many conditions and problems that affect cognitive ability as well as physical and emotional wellbeing.

These include difficulties with:

- Tracking a moving object with the eyes or moving the eyes from one spot to another. This can make it hard to read, catch a ball etc.

- Bumping into people and things or falling off steps.

- Protecting yourself when falling. You might not know which way you are going to fall, or not realise you should put your hands out to protect yourself.

- Sitting still on a chair or working efficiently at a desk.

- Lining up two things together in space, for example, sticking one thing onto another.

- Spacing letters when writing.

- Dancing or playing hopscotch and other games that require movement and co-ordination.

- Using and manipulating tools safely and efficiently.

- Riding a bike.

- Spatial awareness, including not knowing how close you are standing to others.

- Anxiety in large open spaces, fear of getting lost.

(Adapted from Daly and O'Connor 2009)

Motor planning

Linked to a lot of these difficulties is 'motor planning', also known as 'praxis'.

Ayres' definition for this is 'the ability to plan and carry out an unfamiliar action' (Ayres 2005:87). This might be a physical task the child has never had to attempt before, or a familiar task done in a new way. Not only does it involve adapting to the new situation, but it also enables learning how to ultimately perform the task automatically, without having to think about it or to look at the relevant body parts in order to be able to do it.

Moving well

Before we consider the problems that some children may have with motor planning, let's consider what 'moving well' means. It involves:

- Being balanced and stable in movement.

- Having a good sense of body awareness.

- Being able to control the body as it moves.

- Ensuring smooth movement through co-ordination of different body parts.

- Gauging strength and speed correctly.

- Good awareness of directionality.

- Careful and efficient manipulation of tools and objects.

- Rhythmic fluency and easy repetition of movements.

- Careful assessment and sound judgement of risk and safety in movement, e.g. knowing your limits and keeping yourself safe, whilst being prepared to stretch yourself and take physical risks.

- The ability to be still and not move, through choice or on demand. (We will explore 'not moving' more deeply in the next section.)

(Adapted from Macintyre 2009:4)

Macintyre notes that the above competencies depend on being able to:

- Pay attention

- Remember what to do

- Use feedback from one attempt to improve the next try.

All of which makes movement tasks that we take for granted, like climbing the stairs, running downhill, getting dressed, using a spoon, doing the housework, carrying things or even just going for a walk, all seem quite complicated! We can also see where the 'planning' comes into it, although once we can do something easily and have physical mastery of it, then it becomes an automatic action, seemingly without any need for thought or 'motor planning'. 'The well-organised brain uses sensory information to plan actions without deliberate thinking, resulting in automatic ease and gracefulness' writes Ayres. She goes on to comment that 'thinking may actually interfere with the spontaneous processing of sensory input and motor responses' (Ayres 2005: 97).

HAVE A THINK ABOUT... MOTOR PLANNING

To get a sense of what is involved in motor planning, think back if you can to when you were learning a new physical skill, such as ballroom dancing, riding a bike, playing the piano, operating an unfamiliar piece of technology or learning to drive.

Think about what was involved in the process and how much concentration you needed to expend in the first instance on the movements involved, getting them in the right order and performing them smoothly.

Then, once you had automatic mastery of the process, consider how your body (and muscle memory) took over the process, leaving you able to perform the task whilst thinking of something else.

Finally, think about what could happen if you started to deliberately think all over again about every aspect of the process even though you can now do it automatically. Even if it didn't make you mess up (and often it does), your brain would be wasting time and energy on thinking about something needlessly, when you could be using it for something else at the same time. It might even compromise your safety (particularly when driving, for example) as it can prevent you from being aware of your environment and alert and ready to respond quickly to threat or danger.

Problems with motor planning

A diagnosis of dyspraxia often follows the recognition that a child has difficulties with motor planning, although, as Ayres (2005) points out, because someone with dyspraxia is poor at motor planning, they often do *too much* motor planning rather than not enough. This is why the task above is helpful in appreciating what it feels like to live with the condition, also known as Developmental Co-ordination Disorder (DCD). The Dyspraxia Foundation provides a very useful definition as follows:

- Developmental Co-ordination Disorder (DCD), also known as dyspraxia, is a common disorder affecting fine and/or gross motor co-ordination in children and adults.

- DCD is formally recognised by international organisations including the World Health Organisation.

- DCD is distinct from other motor disorders such as cerebral palsy and stroke, and occurs across the range of intellectual abilities.

- Individuals may vary in how their difficulties present: these may change over time depending on environmental demands and life experiences, and will persist into adulthood.

- Children may present with difficulties with self-care, writing, typing, riding a bike and play as well as other educational and recreational activities.

The Foundation also recognises that there are non-motor difficulties that people with the condition may experience that can also affect their daily lives, including memory, perception and processing as well as additional problems with planning, organising and carrying out movements in the right order in everyday situations. Although dyspraxia may occur in isolation, it frequently coexists with other conditions such as Attention Deficit Hyperactive Disorder (ADHD), dyslexia, language disorders and social, emotional and behavioural impairments (adapted from The Dyspraxia Foundation 2015).

Indicators of DCD

There are some generally recognised indicators for DCD in young children. These include:

- Poor balance, co-ordination and control – appearing clumsy and awkward, accident prone, falling over a lot

- Hypotonia (low muscle tone)

- Hyperflexibility of the joints

- Difficulty in running, hopping, dealing with stairs, playing with balls etc.

- Struggling with self-help skills like dressing, shoelaces etc. and activities such as puzzles or shape sorting games

- Often anxious and distracted

- Tactile defensiveness – easily irritated by clothes (finds haircuts painful)

- Poor transfer or habituation of movement skills – struggling to use a learned movement pattern in different but similar situations

- Doing things in inefficient ways – leaving out or adding extra steps to the process of an activity.

(Adapted from The Dyspraxia Foundation 2015;
Macintyre 2009; Ayres 2005)

What causes dyspraxia?

There is still some debate about the causes of DCD and The Dyspraxia Foundation considers that for most children and adults with the condition there is no definite known cause, as people with dyspraxia appear to have no clinical neurological abnormality. Research so far suggests that it may be due to an immaturity of neurone development, which Macintyre describes as leading to an 'overabundance' of unwanted neurons and neural networks which the developing system cannot rid itself of and which causes 'faulty processing of perceptual information' (Carlson et al. 1988, cited in Macintyre 2009:11).

Ayres advises that a child dealing with sensory processing or motor planning deficiencies is likely to feel very frustrated and anxious and their behaviour may be challenging as they attempt to convey their distress to us. 'He needs adults to see his world the way he sees it' and she cautions us to 'Let him develop at his own pace as he cannot develop at someone else's pace' and to 'Give him understanding, protection and opportunity at his own level' (Ayres 2005:101).

There are a number of therapies and sources of support available for families with children who may have dyspraxia, so it is crucial that we always seek qualified SEND advice and guidance if we have concerns about a child's motor development.

The time it takes

In a typically developing child the vestibular system takes years to fully develop. 'Training of these systems is a gradual process during which maturation of the vestibular pathways involved will take until at least 7 years of age, and continue through puberty and beyond' Goddard Blythe (2004:17). This has important implications for our expectations of young children, particularly when they arrive in school. Given that the vestibular system plays such an important part in both visual and auditory processing, it is no wonder that some children will find copying from a board (or a word list on a wall) a challenge, and may not be able to hear the distinctions between certain phonic sounds at the age at which they are expected to learn to recognise them. Furthermore, if we know that movement is fundamental to vestibular development, then it seems obvious that children will continue to need lots of opportunity for self-initiated movement up until the age of seven at the very least, if this crucial aspect of physical development is to be fostered and encouraged.

Sitting still

'The most advanced level of movement is the ability to stay totally still' (Rowe 1994–5, cited by Goddard Blythe 2004:137) and you need balance to be able to sit still. Is it perhaps unrealistic of adults, then, to expect children to be able to sit still, long before they have fully developed their 'balance system'? Children as young as three are increasingly finding themselves sitting in groups for 'phonics' teaching or gathered for assemblies when the expectation is that their bodies will sit still while they concentrate and 'pay attention' with their 'heads'. Any group of children organised in this way will largely fall into two groups – those who can sit still and those who can't. Those who can't will soon be made aware of their inability to conform, whilst those who appear to be able to sit still may well be using all their energies on controlling their body, leaving them little brain space left for concentrating on the phonics lesson! In fact, the opportunity to fiddle and fidget about is more likely to enhance concentration, as most adults know for themselves.

As Goddard Blythe reminds us, 'Education should be a continuous process of sensory as well as intellectual training, not an environment for sensory atrophy (sitting still all day long)' (Goddard Blythe 2004:137).

Internal body 'maps'

What is proprioceptive development?

The terms 'proprioception' and 'proprioceptive' come from the Latin word 'proprius' meaning 'one's own'. This helps us appreciate what is involved in proprioception as it provides us with a sense of our own bodily selves – 'a dynamic sensory-motor map of the body' (LeVoguer and Pasch 2014:101) so that we know where our bodies start and finish and where we are in relation to the rest of the world. Connell and McCarthy refer to proprioception as the sense of 'intuition' and liken it to a 'personal global positioning system (GPS), helping you understand your body in relation to your environment' (Connell and McCarthy 2014:90).

We constantly receive sensory information from our 'proprioceptors' – the sensors at every nerve ending in our limbs and our inner ear that provide information about joint angle, muscle contraction and position, helping to create our body maps by sending 'information to the brain about your position in space, your relationship to that space and the current conditions of the environment and objects you encounter' (Connell and McCarthy 2014:90). It's what helps us walk through a narrow doorway without bumping into the doorframe, not by looking, but by an inner sense that helps us judge our position in relation to the space available, so that we can negotiate doorways without giving them much thought. This is an important fact about proprioception – most of the input is processed in parts of the brain that do not produce any conscious awareness. We very rarely notice the sensations of our muscles and joints unless we purposefully pay attention to them. 'Even if we try to be aware, we feel only a small fraction of all the proprioception that is present during movement' (Ayres 2005:41). And yet, as Mickey LeVoguer and Jasmine Pasch, writing in *Exploring Well-being in the Early Years* (2014) point out, it is this information that 'helps children to feel at home in their bodies' (2014:101).

Well-organised body maps

Having adequate development and integration of the proprioceptive system enables us:

■ To 'feel' our bodies more accurately and to have the kind of body awareness that reinforces a sense of 'What do I look like?' 'Where do I start and finish?' and 'What does my body feel like?' both on the outside and the inside. This supports a subconscious sense of self as well as a physical body consciousness.

■ To efficiently process information about the relationship between different parts of our body (e.g. left and right, top and bottom etc.) and how they can work together or separately.

■ To build spatial awareness of how our bodies 'fit' in the space around us.

■ To manage strength and effort efficiently, in the way we interact with the environment, with other people and with objects.

■ To navigate ourselves in the space around us and to plan movements.

When our proprioceptive sense is adequately developed, all this happens automatically whether we are moving or still and even when we are asleep. Our proprioceptors are constantly (and instantly) sending messages to the brain to provide information about our position, and reinforcing the all-important sense of 'feeling at home' in our bodies that allows us to focus on other aspects of daily life.

Proprioception and movement

These messages are also vitally important in helping us with movement. Without them, we would be dependent on vision and touch alone to tell us where our bodies are in relation to the things around us as we move and engage with our environment. This would slow us down dramatically, make us clumsier and involve a great deal more effort.

HAVE A THINK ABOUT... MOVEMENTS AND ACTIONS YOU PROBABLY TAKE FOR GRANTED

■ Sitting down on a chair

■ Getting in and out of a car

■ Walking downstairs carrying a bundle of washing

■ Tying the strings of an apron or doing up buttons or zips behind your back

■ Tying up or plaiting your own hair

■ Taking something out of a pocket

■ Drinking from a cup, eating with utensils or your fingers

■ Walking down the street whilst looking at your phone

As an adult we tend to be able do all these things without the need to look at what our limbs and body parts are doing. When using our hands behind our backs we don't even have a choice – we can't possibly see what our hands and fingers are doing and yet most of us learned how to tie something behind our backs relatively easily, once we had mastered the art of tying knots and bows. As well as proprioceptive signals from our shoulders, arms, hands and fingers, we are guided by 'neural memories' (Ayres 2005:94) of previous experiences.

Are you a 'touch-typer'? If not, you will probably appreciate that you would be able to copy and type faster (and more efficiently) if you didn't have to keep checking the keyboard as well as the screen. But if you have had a lot of experience of typing you will probably be discovering that your fingers seem to have an instinctive memory for where the keys are, even if you don't yet trust them enough not to keep looking at the keyboard. What might this tell us about the proprioceptive system and the way it develops?

Take some time to observe babies and small children moving.

What do their actions tell you about what their bodies are learning from their proprioceptors?

What movements and actions can they not yet perform without looking at their limbs and body parts?

How does this affect the speed and efficiency of their movements?

Poorly organised body maps

Imagine if you, as an adult, had to bring that level of visual focus to every move you make. Ayres describes children with poorly organised proprioception as usually having 'a lot of trouble doing anything when they cannot see it with their eyes' (Ayres 2005:41). This is often the case for children with developmental dyspraxia as they rely upon vision more than children with typical physical development. As well as bumping into things and having accidents more frequently, not being able to process adequate information from the proprioceptors might mean that they have difficulty judging how much muscular effort they need to do something, so they might often break toys etc. when playing with them. It has been suggested (Goddard Blythe 2009) that some children who are scared of the dark or find it difficult to sleep alone may have proprioceptive difficulties. If there is no strong internal sense of the body then it can be unsettling not to be able to see one's own body in the dark, but feeling the touch of someone alongside them, or having a nightlight, reassures the child and enables them to fall asleep. Similarly, some children (and adults) are soothed by weighted blankets that provide reassuring pressure on the limbs, or by sleeping 'cocooned' inside sleeping bags that provide all round tactile sensations.

Building proprioception

Most children will instinctively seek out proprioceptive-building activities. Hopping, jumping, stretching, running, bouncing, are all movement activities that reinforce position and provide the brain with appropriate stimulation. Also valuable is 'heavy work' – pushing, pulling, brushing, sweeping, lifting and carrying; all done in purposeful activities as children build dens, transport things around the setting, rearrange their environment and engage in tidy up jobs and daily chores that have meaning for them and enable them to take responsibility for their environment. Robust and vigorous games like tug of war, swinging and hanging from 'monkey bars' and 'rough and tumble' play are also very important. We will look more closely at this kind of play in Chapter 7 when we explore the value of risk and challenge in young children's physical development. See below for further 'Playful ideas' for supporting proprioceptive development. Although some ideas may seem age-specific, they can also be adapted to suit children at most stages of development within the EYFS and even beyond. Use them spontaneously, responding 'in the moment' to what your observations tell you about a child's developmental readiness, as well as in short bursts of structured activity in small groups, if and when appropriate.

Proprioception and the importance of touch

The tactile sense, experienced through the sensations of touch, is strongly linked to the development of well-organised body maps. Our skin is the largest organ of the body and has nerve sensors that pick up and send information about pressure, heat, cold and pain as well as touch (both heavy and light) and proprioception (Hannaford 2005:44).

There has been a lot of research into the importance of touch in early development, showing that tactile experience is vital not just for physical and emotional wellbeing but also for nerve growth and learning development (Tortora and Anagnostakos 1990; Meaney et al. 1988; Francis and Meaney 1999; Ardiel and Rankin 2010). This includes research into the experiences of premature babies and the advantages of 'kangaroo care' where the baby benefits from time spent 'skin-on-skin' with a parent rather than isolated in an incubator (Pearce 1986).

The importance of touch in 'embodied education'

As discussed in earlier chapters, changes in our childrearing practices have reduced the opportunities for natural and instinctive physical closeness and touch for many of our children. Breastfeeding, co-sleeping and baby sling wearing are all ways that have traditionally increased the amount of daily tactile experiences for babies and young children, but for a variety of reasons these are not always possible for every family. Add to this the generalised heightening of concern about physical and sexual abuse and children are less likely to have physical contact with others outside of their immediate family. Yet the evidence is there to suggest that not just children's physical and emotional wellbeing is affected by a lack of physical contact, but also their learning development as the brain doesn't receive the required early stimulation to support its development.

'Every child should have opportunities for spontaneous, affectionate physical contact every day. Additional experiences, such as massage, can help counteract the effects of our increasing contact-less culture' (Daly and O'Connor 2009).

Support for vestibular and proprioceptive difficulties

Organisations such as the Institute of Neurophysiological Psychology (INPP) and Rhythmic Movement Training (RMT) in the UK (and individual licensed clinicians) provide remediation and treatment for diagnosed difficulties related to vestibular and proprioceptive development. These issues may also be linked to retained reflexes and to trauma experienced during birth or in the early years. Many adoptive and foster families find that as well as attachment issues, their children also experience delays or 'hiccups' in their vestibular and proprioceptive development. However, it is important to stress again that these difficulties can also occur in children in stable families and who have not experienced early trauma. Exercises and activities are tailored to the child's particular needs and reviewed appropriately. Please seek advice if you have concerns about a child's development. The ideas and suggestions below are suitable for all children and aim to replicate and supplement the instinctive and intuitive rich diet of experiences that children naturally engage in, whilst providing the opportunity to fill in some of the 'gaps' that some children may be experiencing.

Partnership with parents

Parents may be less aware of the vestibular and proprioceptive senses than they are of the other senses:

- Consider ways to provide them with information that will be most appropriate for your community of parents.

- Explore with them the value of a daily diet of movement play activities that stimulate vestibular and proprioceptive development.

- Consider running workshops that offer opportunities for sensory activities, particularly messy play, that reduce their anxieties and increase their awareness of the role of these activities in learning and all round development.

- For parents experiencing sleep issues with their children, offer them information about how proprioception may play a part in this and suggest ways they could address this as mentioned above.

Partnership with other professionals

Other professionals and staff working with older children also may not have had much information about these areas in their training.

■ Think about ways you can offer to share new information and understanding, perhaps through skill share sessions.

■ Ensure that records, observations and children's learning journals include information on their vestibular and proprioceptive development, and be prepared to explain the relevance of this to children's future learning and progress.

Summary

The vestibular and proprioceptive sensory systems are extremely important features of a child's physical development as they contribute to a wide range of aspects of learning, as well as physical and emotional wellbeing.

Some children may experience gaps in their vestibular and proprioceptive development that can affect their progress in motor skills and specific learning, as well as their communication, behaviour and emotional development.

Implications for practice

■ Children will instinctively develop their vestibular and proprioceptive senses through playful movement experiences and activities, but we need to provide an early years environment that is rich in these opportunities to ensure that all children have as much of this experience as possible.

■ The vestibular and proprioceptive senses benefit most from self-initiated activities that are driven by the child's own motivations. Stimulating and supporting this inner drive for sensory development has to be a main priority of early childhood care and education if we are to support all later learning development and wellbeing.

■ Some children's behaviours may be driven by their gaps in sensory development and our responses to children's behaviour should reflect this awareness. Equally, our growing understanding of the role played by these key senses should enable us to observe and assess children's physical development more accurately, seeking professional guidance and advice where necessary and signposting parents to available help and support.

■ Using new information about the links between language and vestibular development, practitioners should consider engaging in action research to explore alternative ways of promoting and supporting speech and language development.

Playful ideas: for supporting vestibular and proprioceptive development

Some of the following activities specifically support either the vestibular system or proprioception, although some cover both bases! Activities that involve 'heavy' work like pushing, pulling, carrying etc. are good for proprioception, as are games and resources that involve touch and tactile sensations with different parts of the body. Use them spontaneously, responding 'in the moment' to what your observations tell you about a child's developmental readiness, as well as in short bursts of structured activity in small groups, if and when appropriate.

Roundabouts. Try spinning in different positions – sitting, on knees, on one side, on tummy, standing, with eyes closed, with someone else holding hands or being swung round (hold under the arms or round belly). Enjoy the sensations of stopping as much as the spinning. Explore changes of pace and direction of spin.

Swings. Hold children under the arms or round the middle and swing side to side or forwards and backwards. Make sure to look after your own body as you do this, with a wide stance and bent knees to protect your back.

Slides. Do body slides along the floor, on bottoms, tummies or backs. Try using fabric, plastic or vinyl taped to the floor to make a slidey surface. Or drag someone along on the fabric. They can sit or lie on tummies, bottoms or backs. Push someone along the floor as you slide yourself – pushing with your legs or gently pulling along with arms or legs.

Dancing scarves. Cut up strips of cheap lining fabric or voile to make scarves that will support a wide variety of playful and creative activities. The scarves can be twirled and flapped and are great stimulus for dancing – spinning and twirling the body along with the scarves. Imagine the scarves to be colours with which you can paint the whole space in stripes, polka dots and large swirls of paint! Some children like to drape themselves in the scarves and tie them around their waists.

To me, to you. With something solid, e.g. a box or filled washing basket between you, take turns pushing and pulling to and fro. Try with the child standing, allowing them to keep in contact all the time so they can sense the change and help their balance.

Popcorn. Put some light balls on a big piece of lycra and let them bounce around. Catch the balls and throw back on, settle the balls and the lycra and then go for a crawl about on top of it.

Obstacle course. With support if needed, explore stepping and clambering on and over different obstacles. Make yourself an obstacle to be negotiated and crawled over.

Horsey rides. If you are comfortable with it (and your children aren't too large!) let them ride on your back as you slowly crawl on all fours. (Kneepads make it more comfortable for adults to crawl.) See how different children react, engage and risk assess this game. With your own body and kinaesthetic sense, can you notice how the confident child or the scared child feels when engaging with this game?

Stair crawling. We all know how small children love to try to master the obstacles of stairs and steps. If you have access to safe and clean stairs and outdoor steps, use them for exploring different ways of getting up and down. This is an opportunity for lots of physical processing and problem solving, while the grown up stays close, carefully watching and encouraging.

Cushion mountain. Create a pile of cushions and pillows that can be crawled and climbed over by babies. Hide on the other side to provide a bit of motivation to come find you. Fantastic for physical co-ordination, strength and proprioception. Great sense of achievement too!

Make a 'child sandwich' out of cushions with the child as the filling. Gentle pressure and lots of pretend 'eating' noises make this a fun and giggly game.

Sweeping with brooms, both adult and child-sized, is an excellent activity for proprioception as well as involving children with tidying and cleaning. Make the most of puddles when it rains and encourage sweeping up the water.

Weighted cushions, blankets and stuffed toys are now easily available to purchase and can also be made fairly cheaply.

Some of these ideas are adapted from Masi and Cohen Leiderman (2004).

7 Physical development and the EYFS

This chapter focuses on the role of physical development in early learning and its importance within current curriculum guidance. More children are experiencing day care and early education outside the home than ever before, with a government drive to introduce children as young as two years old into school environments. This means that settings are well placed to provide intervention and support to enhance children's physical development. However, it also means that we carry a professional responsibility to ensure that our practice and curriculum do not hinder or damage children's biological drive for physical mastery and agency in their own development. Although specific reference is made to the Statutory Framework for the Early Years Foundation Stage (EYFS) in England, the main thrust of this chapter focuses on the guiding principles that should underpin all curriculum practice, regardless of location or current government guidelines.

Physical Development as a Prime area

Changes to the EYFS in 2012 included the creation of three Prime areas together with four Specific areas.

The creation of the Prime areas is an important development as it gives weight to the understanding that they are crucial to our physical and emotional wellbeing as well as to all later learning. As Helen Moylett and Nancy Stewart explain in *Understanding the Revised Early Years Foundation Stage* (2012) the Prime areas are universally 'time-sensitive'. If they are 'not securely in place between 3–5 years, they will be more difficult to acquire and their absence may hold the child back in other areas of learning' (Moylett and Stewart 2012:19). It's important to make the point here that the emphasis is not that they cannot be acquired later, but that it becomes much more difficult. So why make it more difficult?

Moylett and Stewart also comment on the fact that the Prime areas are *universal*. This means they occur in all communities and cultures, whereas the Specific areas don't, or at least not in the same ways – they are *specific* to the priorities held by different communities and cultures and 'reflect cultural knowledge and accumulated understanding' within those communities. Moreover, the Prime areas are not dependent on the Specific areas of learning, but 'the specific learning cannot easily take place without the prime' (Moylett and Stewart 2012:19).

Learning *about* movement and learning *through* movement

'Moving to learn and learning to move are key to the child's overall development' (Maude 2001:26).

This is a statement we believe to be fundamental to our practice with young children. Children need specific activities to promote their knowledge and understanding of their own bodies and how they work. This starts in the earliest of years when we play games with babies, pointing out their nose and ears and tickling their tummies. It continues right through to them becoming more physically literate, when they begin to understand aspects of physical education, such as the way the heart rate increases with exercise and that there are optimum ways to throw a ball or jump over a hurdle. But we must also pay attention to the fact that children learn *through* movement, whether in specific ways (see below) or because their earliest movement experiences lay down foundations in the brain and body that 'prime' them for all the learning that is to follow.

Physical development and the Specific areas

Let's now turn our attention to the Specific areas and consider the often forgotten role that physical development plays in each of them, bearing in mind that the Specific areas 'all depend on competence within the prime areas' (Pound 2013:69). This means that children's development in the Specific areas cannot proceed well unless they have had sufficient experience and opportunities to develop physically, emotionally and linguistically. Just as importantly, where opportunities are provided for children to explore the Specific areas as part of their imaginative play, they also in turn support a child's physical development.

Physical development and Mathematics

Spatial awareness / positional and directional language – movement is important in a child's exploration and understanding of space and themselves within it, and their understanding of positional language (in, on, under, behind etc.) depends upon it. This has a direct link with 'whole body awareness' of the complexities of directional language and directional reasoning which is the 'understanding of how two objects relate to each other in space' and underpins academic skills of literacy as well as maths (Connell and McCarthy 2014:173).

Using the fingers to count is commonly seen in the early stages of numeracy development, bringing an important, physical, multi-sensory element to the experience of making sense of counting and numbers. We shouldn't dismiss it as a childish function, however; outside the Western hemisphere advanced techniques for finger counting are learnt by children and put to very good use as aids for calculating large and complex amounts.

Gross motor activities often readily lend themselves to counting and ordering – whilst stepping, climbing stairs, swinging, starting a physical activity with '1, 2, 3 go!' as well as physical problem solving, sequencing and repetition of movements/ action in a pattern.

Fine motor activities are an essential part of early mathematical exploration – manipulating items (natural and manufactured) for counting and sorting, as well as control of writing tools for later recording. All of the 'fine motor skills' that are linked with any of the Specific areas, have their origins in gross motor movement (Pound 2013:78).

Block play is crucial for early mathematical development – and involves both fine and gross motor activity in lifting, carrying, manipulating, and exploring position and directionality. Length, volume, fractions, capacity, as well as problem solving and creativity, also feature in small and large block play, as does working in both 2D and 3D and involving more than one directional plane.

Playful movement should be an essential feature of early mathematical exploration as children engage in imaginative play, problem solving and making things for their own purposes.

HAVE A THINK ABOUT... THE COMPLEXITIES OF DIRECTIONAL LANGUAGE

How many common phrases can you think of that use the word 'in'?

- In trouble

- Get in

- In mind

- In hope

- In an argument

- In the house

- In amazement

- In fact

- In love

- Come on in

■ In case

■ In summer, winter etc.

The most obvious meaning (and the one that we most commonly think we are teaching children) is the situation of something enclosed or surrounded by something else. But children are actually hearing a wide range of uses of the word and have to move beyond the literal sense in order to understand how the same word can convey a 'sense' of position, but with a wide variety of actual meanings. Words like 'in' that are used in idiomatic phrases are 'directional concepts' that require us to understand and appreciate the context in which they are used, before we can understand their meaning. The more physical experience children have, the more they can make sense of the meaning through context.

Make a list of other directional words and think of the different ways we use them.

How do you ensure a rich variety of contexts for children to experience directional language?

(Adapted from Connell and McCarthy 2014:164–168)

Physical development and Expressive Arts and Design

A wide range of physical activity is involved in all aspects of Expressive Arts and Design at whatever stage of development – from basic finger painting and hand printing to playing musical instruments that demand different parts of the body move in different ways at different times.

Expressive movement can be spontaneous or contained and channelled – young children express delight in themselves, their bodies and their world through spontaneous movements, from the baby waving their arms, kicking their feet and wiggling their toes as a familiar adult approaches, to the five-year-old jumping up and down and clapping their hands with glee whilst listening to an exciting story. Older and/or more physically experienced children are increasingly able to contain and channel their expressive movements, e.g. through dance, gymnastics, art or design, although the will to spontaneously respond to stimuli hopefully remains active throughout life.

Making things is a fundamental part of Expressive Arts and Design and obviously gross and fine motor skills are key to this – from building a den to manipulating play dough, from junk modelling with big cardboard boxes to playing with Lego bricks and cutting out intricate patterns with scissors, all involve a range of motor skills that become increasingly refined the more physical experience a child has and the more their imagination is fired and the urge to create is fostered and promoted.

Imaginative play is rarely still – it involves the whole body as children 'inhabit' their favourite superhero or mimic the actions of their parent in the home corner or their teacher as they play 'school' out in the garden. Whether the actions are robust and vigorous as superheroes rush around saving the world, or contained and gentle as mummies and daddies tend to their babies in their prams – imaginative play and movement are inextricably linked. If children's opportunities for imaginative play are restricted or inhibited, then they will be missing valuable opportunities for physical development.

HAVE A THINK ABOUT... CHILDREN'S PHYSICAL RESPONSES TO STORIES

We often encourage children to join in with stories and songs through planned movement and 'actions' but how easy is it for children to spontaneously respond in a physical way to your storytelling?

Is there space for them to sit, kneel, stand, and lie down while they listen?

Can they jump up, reach out, wave their arms, and clap their hands in individual response to the story?

Do you tell stories outside? On the move, whilst walking around the garden, the park, down the street? Have you tried telling a 'promenade' story where each section takes place in a different space, giving children the chance to move around on their way to the next part of the story?

Not all stories have to be active, and young children will often sit quite still and enraptured for a well-told tale, but be open to the possibilities of using stories to promote and trigger movement and dance experiences.

Physical development and Understanding the World

This Specific area covers learning sometimes described as the humanities (history and geography) as well as science and technology.

Finding out about people and communities involves physical action – real life activities that reflect what is familiar in the child's life as well as what is unfamiliar, in order for them to learn about and appreciate the world as it is lived by other people, whether they live in the same street or another hemisphere.

First-hand experience is fundamental to this – not just sitting at a desk finding out about it from a book or screen. It involves being out and about in the local area, as well as trips further afield (as appropriate), meeting people, shopping, cooking, playing with artefacts, listening and responding to music of different rhythms and beat. Sometimes photographs, film or computer images *are* useful as they show children something they might otherwise not experience. However, what is important is having the opportunity and encouragement to respond physically to what they are seeing or hearing – to dance along, or physically engage in some way with the unfamiliar experience, enabling it to become more meaningful. As an example, a clip from the observational film *The Power of Physical Play* (Siren Films 2014) shows young boys in a nursery class dancing along to a video of Irish dancers whilst wearing donated Irish dancing costumes (dresses). The sensations of moving, feeling the weight of the fabric as they swirl and jump to the music, provides the boys with kinaesthetic empathy. This 'felt sense' allows the boys to relate to what they are seeing in a more powerful, embodied way. The link was local, in that the costumes belonged to the family of someone in the setting, but for many of the children it provided the opportunity to engage physically with a positive cultural activity outside of their usual experience. It gave them a chance to see what it feels like to be 'in someone else's shoes', which is an important element of cultural understanding.

Forces and energy are something that children first find out about through their bodies and physical action. Pushing, pulling, sliding and falling all tell them a lot about forces and the way they impact on them, particularly once they incorporate objects into their play.

Technology and young children is more of a controversial issue as many commentators express concern that children are exposed to screen technology, in particular, at increasingly young ages. There is still some debate as to whether the technology from phones and other Wi-Fi enabled equipment may prove harmful to young bodies and brains (The Connexion 2015). However, there is also a justified anxiety that screens not only encourage sedentary activity and take away from time that children could be spending in more physically active experiences, they also don't provide children with the rich sensory feedback their bodies and brains need for development. As Steiner practitioners point out, there is a difference between the kind of technological devices (e.g. tablets, TVs, computers) of which most adults don't even understand the workings, and those that enable and encourage small children to figure out and understand how they work for themselves (e.g. can opener, egg whisk). Dis-assembling things (e.g. old radios, vacuum cleaners, keyboards), whether or not you re-assemble them, triggers physical problem solving and investigation, providing sensory feedback and the desire to learn more.

HAVE A THINK ABOUT... CHILDREN AND SCREEN TECHNOLOGY

Some educationalists believe that children need to become efficient users of screen technology as early as possible, encouraging the use of computers, interactive whiteboards and tablets with very young children. Others believe that even if children aren't already accustomed to using them at home, they will receive plenty of exposure to them throughout KS1, 2 and 3, and that the early years should be left free for other activities that may be denied to them as they get older (e.g. sand and water and other kinds of sensory play).

What is your opinion on the use of technology in the early years? What do you know about the arguments for and against?

Do you feel pressure to use screens and computers in your setting or are you an 'eager early adopter' of new technologies?

How confident are you in using information technology with young children to ensure it is purposeful and suitable for their interests and developmental stages?

What safeguards do you have in place to ensure children are not spending too much time on sedentary activities in your setting?

Do you use television, DVDs and radios in your setting?

How do you work with parents to support them in their understanding of the potential risks associated with too much screen time and sedentary activity?

Physical development and Literacy

Physical development and movement play have a significant contribution to make towards literacy development.

Exploring stories physically enhances the experience for children – strengthening their interest in literature and helping to embed stories and literary conventions through an experiential process. **There are a range of reflexes** and early movement experiences that make a significant contribution to literacy development – building hand-eye coordination, pencil grip, visual tracking etc.

Development of cross-laterality – enabling children to read and write (in English) from left to right.

Understanding of directionality – linked to whole body and spatial awareness (as in Maths) e.g. knowing that print books have a front and a back, print begins and ends in different places, and skips down and across from the end of one line to the beginning of another, pages turn and are read in a specific direction depending on the language used (Connell and McCarthy 2014).

Fine motor control is required for competent, comfortable handwriting, keyboard use etc. and depends on the development of earlier gross motor skills.

The fingers often play an important part in early reading – providing 'a scouting party for the eyes, keeping the eyes on track and flowing from word to word' (Connell and McCarthy 2014:137). This is helpful because a child beginning to read doesn't always have the 'visual figure grounding' essential for ignoring everything apart from the words they are attempting to read, as well as the peripheral vision required to point the way forward to the next piece of text on the page. The finger moving along the line of words provides the physical 'scaffolding' the child needs until the eyes (and brain) are experienced enough in reading to not need it anymore. It also allows the child to focus on the meaning of the words rather than the 'physical mechanics' (Connell and McCarthy 2014:137) of moving the eyes along the row of words.

HAVE A THINK ABOUT... SUPPORTING SPECIFIC LITERACY DEVELOPMENT THROUGH PHYSICAL DEVELOPMENT AND MOVEMENT PLAY

Make a list of all the physical activities and experiences you regularly offer that support literacy. Include everything, no matter how small or seemingly unrelated to reading or writing, and take photographs of those activities in action.

Now ask yourself...

Are there *any* physical activities and experiences that don't ultimately support reading and writing in some way or another?

Crossing curriculum boundaries

It is worth reminding ourselves here of some of the principles mentioned in Chapter 1. If 'movement is the primary means by which concepts are experienced' (Manners 2015b) then it is also very often a strong connecting feature across all areas of the curriculum, linking one with another and crossing all curriculum boundaries. A further principle, 'PD skills are transferable and should have meaning in all aspects of a child's life' (Manners 2015b) reinforces this, as well as reminding us that young children don't tend to learn in 'curriculum categories'. Much of the information above with regard to the Specific areas crosses curriculum boundaries and can be applied to all areas of learning, regardless of current curriculum guidance or legislation.

Structured programmes

Sadly the significance of physical development's contribution to the Specific areas remains largely overlooked. This is especially true when it comes to understanding the length of time children need for their bodies to mature before they are capable of, in particular, some of the fine motor literacy skills that are now demanded of them at ever earlier ages. What understanding there is has led to the appearance of structured programmes aimed at supporting literacy development specifically through dance or movement. Although the connection is an important one, Linda Pound notes that 'such programmes appear to be popular amongst practitioners but evaluation is limited and inconclusive' and that a 'further drawback is that no matter how enticing activities of this sort are they take time away from the spontaneous activity through which children get in touch with their own bodies' (Pound 2013:74).

Physical scribbling

Early years practitioners understand well the value of scribbling and random mark-making across all areas of the curriculum, whether it be early drawings and pretend writing of letters and numbers done with writing tools or with fingers in the sand or dipped in paint. The scribbling process is seen as vital in enabling the child to explore not only the tools and media but also their own abilities to make marks and representations that carry meaning for them, even if the grownups have to have them explained. 'Physical scribbling' needs to be recognised as having the same importance.

'Just as we encourage and understand a child's scribbles and marks as pre-writing skills and explorations, so the same can be said for physical play and lots of wriggling and fidgeting! It all needs to be worked out, repeated and improved before other skills can develop that will lead to successful writing, reading, communication and physical mastery' (Daly and O'Connor 2009). This means providing lots of opportunities for honouring children's physical scribbles and their drive to move, to fidget and wriggle and not be still, especially when concentrating, thinking, talking, problem solving, creating and exploring. Of necessity this must also involve lots of open-ended play, indoors and out, with accessible, open-ended equipment and resources, where children can wallow in ideas and express themselves through movement of all kinds.

Without those opportunities we run the risk of stifling natural development and putting in its place a surface level of 'achievement' that doesn't include the drive and motivation to want to pursue learning above and beyond whatever statutory goals are currently in place. Vivian Gussin Paley reminds us of the value of honouring children's instinctive drive to learn by creating for them 'an early school experience that best represents the natural development of young children' (Paley 2004:8, cited in Pound 2013:74).

How dance supports the EYFS curriculum

Although dance is contained within the Specific area of Expressive Arts and Design, we feel that it deserves some special consideration, as a medium for physical development and also as a primary support for all aspects of the EYFS curriculum. Dance 'is intrinsically linked to our early physical development, as young children experiment with movement responses to the stimulus of the world around them' (Daly and O'Connor 2013). Young children dancing should not have any of the inhibitions or hang-ups that beset adults, specifically because an early years environment should always provide an encouraging and non-judgemental atmosphere that enables children to readily explore their responses to music and other stimuli. This includes dancing just for the sheer fun and joy of it and to glory in the physical sensations of moving to music.

Physical development

Clearly dance is closely linked to physical development as it supports sensory integration and is particularly relevant to the growth of the vestibular and proprioceptive systems. The urge to dance, especially to music, motivates and encourages healthy activity, exercising gross and fine motor skills and developing positive associations with the physical self.

Personal, social, and emotional development

In PSED, dance encourages resilience and problem solving, either through learning steps or working through a personal response to a stimulus. It is often a social and cultural activity that brings with it a feel-good factor, as people come together either to watch or join in. It is worth mentioning that the existence of 'mirror neurons' allows our brains to benefit from watching others dancing (and engaging in physical activity) almost as much as if we were doing it ourselves. This is an important feature of brain development, though sadly it doesn't mean we can burn off calories by watching the Olympics, just that our brains benefit from the sensory experience (Berrol 2006). Dance can also facilitate self-expression, and even very young children are capable of interpreting a sad, angry or happy dance.

Communication and language

The links between dance and self-expression are also relevant to the development of communication and language, with the strong emphasis on non-verbal communication within dance. The notion of 'movement conversations' is particularly significant in dance and can provide a powerful way of connecting with children who are reluctant talkers or speak a first language other than English. Dancing reinforces aspects of rhythm and structure, which are important for language and as previously discussed in Chapter 6, movement can encourage vocalisation in some children. Twirling and spinning stimulates the vestibular sense, which in turn can help stimulate the language systems in the brain.

Mathematics

Rhythm and structure are also an important feature of early mathematical exploration, as children explore patterns of beats and timing in their dances. Repetition, ordering and sequencing are also key aspects of mathematics that are reinforced through dance, as well as counting and ordering. Music and maths have very close connections, although it is important to point out that dance doesn't always have to be accompanied by music, although it is often a stimulus for it. Spatial awareness too is developed and strengthened as children make safe use of space and embody a physical understanding of shape and size.

Expressive arts and design

Dance is a major element of this area of the curriculum, particularly as it promotes and encourages creativity. Dance includes the three key areas of improvisation, performing and appreciation, which each have relevance to all areas of expressive arts. Improvisation is particularly important in the early years, as children spontaneously explore moves and patterns of movement to create their own dance sequences. Performance also has its place, though at this age it is much more about having an interested audience of one or two, rather than a meticulously rehearsed performance on stage in front of a crowd (Daly and O'Connor 2013).

Understanding the world

As well as the opportunity to find out about and explore music and dance from around the world and within the local community, dance also reinforces early exploration of forces and energy. This happens particularly when children dance together, feeling each other's weight and the way their bodies support or pull against each other, as they hold hands or swing themselves around. Circle dances and games provide an early experience of 'community' and what it feels like to be part of a group.

Dance and literacy

Once again, beat and rhythm are useful aspects of dance that support reading development. The gross motor movements involved in dancing also support the development of the fine motor skills needed for writing. Visual perception is strengthened by the vestibular activity of dancing, and bilaterality and cross-laterality are reinforced by the movement of different parts of the body, together, separately or with props such as dancing scarves. (See the More Information section.)

A physically rich environment

In relation to physical development, the environment has the same requirements that it has for all early learning. In no particular order, and reduced to the simplest of terms, these are:

- Space
- Time
- People
- Stuff.

How much space is enough space?

This can be a tricky question, particularly as many of us still find ourselves working in cramped or inappropriate spaces that don't seem to lend themselves to a great deal of physical activity. There are minimum legal requirements but these rarely take into account the reality of working with babies and young children. Luckily early years practitioners are known for their versatility and flexible thinking, proving themselves capable of creating stimulating and nurturing environments from the most dispiriting of spaces. Huge amounts of space aren't always helpful either, particularly if they make supervision difficult. Perhaps one of the best ways of improving the quality of physical activity indoors is to remove some of the furniture (or even all!) as tables and chairs are the least helpful items for promoting good physical development. Children will have years of their life left to learn how to sit and work at a table (should they need to) and there is increasing evidence to suggest that traditional seating does not always provide the most effective working conditions. Flooring of different textures, cushions of different sizes and versatile storage and benches can create open-ended spaces that are adaptable for a wide range of uses and encourage children to play on their tummies and move around on their hands and knees, providing valuable physical experiences.

The time it takes

An environment that supports children's physical development provides them with enough time to:

■ Observe others moving and engaging in physical activities of all kinds;

■ 'Have a go' with no notions of fixed or correct outcomes;

■ Make mistakes;

■ Revisit and refine movements and physical actions purposefully in their self-initiated play, to gain automatic mastery of skills and tool use;

■ Play alone and with others, including adults and children younger and older than them;

■ Experience enough frustration to drive problem solving and perseverance, together with sufficient success and satisfaction to encourage motivation and extended learning.

People and relationships

A movement rich environment also relies on physically responsive adults to support, encourage and motivate children's physical activity. This doesn't mean we all have to be Olympic standard athletes, but it does demand a professional responsibility to be knowledgeable about physical development. This means knowing our children well enough to be able to 'tune into' their neurophysiological needs as well as a firm commitment to raising their levels of physical activity 'through encouragement, by following their lead and responding to their innovative ways of moving' (Archer and Siraj 2015:30).

The right stuff

In her book *Resources for Early Learning: Children, Adults and Stuff* (1996) Pat Gura uses the term 'stuff' as shorthand for all the different kinds of resources and equipment used in children's play. These can be natural, hand-made, manufactured or recycled and she reminds us that children will use anything in their play – all you need is a hood on your coat and you can save the world as your favourite superhero (Gura 1996). Superheroes in particular have a lot to contribute to movement and physical play, although we may still need to remind ourselves that vigorous movement activity isn't the only form of play to support physical development.

■ Just about any form of play will involve movement of some kind. Even pretending to be asleep in the home corner bed will be exercising the vestibular and proprioceptive systems as the child 'works' to lie still under the covers!

■ Accessibility is the key to enabling children to explore materials and resources for their own purposes and to enable them to tidy and put things back again when they have finished with them (with help from the grownups).

■ Resources that replicate home experience of tools, utensils and equipment provide children with opportunities to develop domestic and self-help skills that simultaneously reinforce proprioception, e.g. sweeping, pouring, scrubbing, folding, lifting, carrying, washing, stirring, kneading, rolling, cutting, chopping, to name just a few!

■ Although vast empty concrete playgrounds are not especially conducive to developmentally appropriate physical play, there can be a temptation to fill outdoor spaces with so much equipment (often fixed) that children are left with little opportunity for their imaginations to fire their movement play, as well as not leaving enough space for vigorous activity. Ideally, outdoor spaces should provide the kinds of activity that can't be replicated indoors, which means interaction with the natural environment, the weather and any resources that benefit from larger open spaces.

■ There are some resources specifically designed to support aspects of physical development, e.g. body spinning cones. You will find these resources available on special needs websites but remember they are valuable for all children (see More Information). By and large, the best equipment is open-ended. For example,

'A frames' and planks can be arranged and re-arranged by children and adults together to create a whole variety of climbing, sliding and balancing activities, matched to children's experience and skill levels. Static slides and climbing frames have their uses, but most children will experience these in parks and public places – and they can be hard to adapt in order to reduce or increase risk and challenge as appropriate.

■ Opportunities for music making and dancing are imperative in a movement rich environment. Provide CD /MP3 players that can be used outside and in, along with a wide range of music reflecting both the local community and the wider world, as well as contemporary and classical tunes that encourage a variety of movement and dance. A mix of homemade and manufactured musical instruments, ideally some made from natural materials, will encourage both vigorous and quiet music making, important for motor skill development as well as accompanying the dancing!

Risks, hazards and challenge

For some time now, early years specialists have drawn our attention to the difference between 'risk' and 'hazards'. In *Too Safe for Their Own Good*, Jennie Lindon describes a hazard as 'a physical situation that could potentially be harmful'. A risk, however, is 'the probability that the potential harm from this hazard will occur' (Lindon 2011:5). This means that levels of risk will not always be the same for all children, or at different stages of their development. As Lindon points out, 'Risk assessment matters but a sensible process involves consideration of the genuine level of risk, the likely consequences if something does go wrong and the seriousness of those consequences should they occur' (Lindon 2011:6). Furthermore, we have to acknowledge that there can be no such thing as a totally risk free environment – and that we would be failing children if we attempted to create one. An environment that doesn't encourage a degree of risk-taking is actually more likely to create unsafe children who aren't able to think for themselves before attempting something risky, who don't see where potential hazards might lie and who don't develop the resilience and strategic thinking needed to keep themselves 'safe enough' (Tovey 2014) when there are no adults around to do it for them. Our job as practitioners and parents is ultimately to equip children to manage their own risk assessment.

An ill-fitting carpet that everyone might trip over is a hazard that can (and should) be eliminated, but equipment and resources also need to be constantly reviewed and assessed in the light not just of 'safety', but also of the amount of challenge and stimulation they provide.

Fear of litigation

We have a tendency to blame an overly cautious 'health and safety' climate for the reduction in natural risk in children's play experiences. However, this isn't very helpful, given the numbers of children who are alive and unharmed as a result of improved safety conditions. At the same time, a fear of litigation has arisen that has greatly influenced policy-making and encouraged a climate of anxiety and over-caution, influencing practitioners and parents alike. We need to be clear about the value and importance of appropriate risk and challenge to children's all round development and their physical development in particular. In pointing out the role of Vygotsky's (1978) zone of proximal development in our understanding of children's learning, LeVoguer and Pasch comment that not allowing this kind of play could be as potentially damaging to children's development as exposing them to too much risk. If learning occurs when children are able to move to the edge of their current knowledge, then 'inhabiting the edge of physical experience includes taking a risk and facing the unknown' (LeVoguer and Pasch 2014:103). Tim Gill, a very prominent commentator on the subject of risk and children's play, reminds us that there are 'significant forces' urging us towards risk aversion, but that where people have been successful in resisting these forces it is because 'they have an explicit philosophy, ethos or set of values about the role of risk, experiential learning and autonomy in children's lives. The challenge for public policy is to learn from these' (Gill 2007:74).

Daring

Writing about pre-schools in Japan, Daniel J. Walsh describes being fascinated by Japanese children's 'daring' and their fearlessness in attempting physical activity, which he considered outside the norm for this age group. 'They appeared ready to climb to the top of anything' (Walsh 2004:102). He comments on how he began to understand over time that though they seemed daring to him, 'the daring moment masked the gradual process of becoming daring. The daring of five year olds had begun when they were toddlers and had been developed slowly and with much practice' (Walsh 2004:102). Neither the children nor their teachers judged their actions to be daring or dangerous, because they had been performing them in some form or another since they had been toddlers. He notes that Japanese pre-schools generally allow children extended periods of free play outside and that their playgrounds include challenging equipment and unrestricted space in which children can test themselves and the use of equipment. They are given the time and the space to practise and persevere with tasks and activities that physically challenge them.

Developing a sense of daring is a process of continual small steps over a long period of time. The young Japanese self is seen as, and accepted as, a physical self, developed on the playgrounds and in rambunctious interaction with others from an early age.

(Walsh 2004:102)

Figure 7.1 Orla shows no fear in climbing to the top of the stairs.

Rough and tumble

An example of 'rambunctious interaction' is what we are more likely to refer to as 'rough and tumble'. This is the kind of play that most resembles the play of animals and as such it has many purposes including physical problem solving, managing aggression, socialising and assimilating into groups, and learning to accept defeat graciously (LeVoguer and Pasch 2014). It involves body contact with others and includes rolling, wrestling, wriggling, jostling, pushing, pulling, dodging and falling. From a physical development perspective it is invaluable in developing proprioception, sensory integration and risk assessment. It allows us to work both with and against the bodies of others and to develop skills of physical negotiation as well as 'standing our ground'. It is understandable that adults will have safety concerns about children engaging in this kind of play. As always, professional common sense is essential – risk assessments need to be done and we need to be alert for potential hazards and dangers. We also have a professional responsibility to ensure that all children have access to this crucial physical experience at levels of interaction that are exactly right for them. Therefore we need to use our observation skills as key people to ensure that we tune into our children and their individual stages of physical and sensory development. The following should help you plan safely for rough and tumble play.

Making space

Make sure the numbers of bodies and nature of movement play are suited to the space you have, or choose to use. Keep vigorous play clear of furniture and other obstructions, but it doesn't have to be a 'soft' or padded space. Children need to learn to negotiate different surfaces and to develop their own risk assessment around them. Make the most of outdoors and the natural environment for this kind of play.

Supervising

Always supervise physical activities but resist over-policing and getting in the way of potentially exciting explorations. Think about how and where you position yourself to support this kind of play. Are you an observer or an integral part of the play experience? Both are valid. Try to encourage and guide without being too anxious or abruptly ending activities if they get too energetic. Find alternative ways of redirecting or extending the action, for example, through role play.

Don't provide all the answers! Use your knowledge of individual children to know when to stand by and give encouragement while they negotiate tricky situations or find out how to right themselves after a bump or trip.

Be aware of dynamics and the intentions behind children's movements – it is often seen as rude or aggressive when a child becomes physically engrossed in a movement or sensation, yet we wouldn't distract them if they were equally engrossed in a writing task, for example.

Can you spot the difference between aggressively out-of-control behaviour and imaginative, fully engaged physical contact? Be aware of children who get over-excited or particularly stressed by lots of physical play. Find a smaller 'bite-sized' way of playing with them, and carefully monitor their development.

Also be aware of children who are wary of close contact with others. Find ways of building their confidence and making the sensation feel safe. Try using fabric or scarves for pulling and tugging (e.g. playing see-saw games or 'horse'), allowing children to join in with a level of sensation that works for them.

Getting involved

One of the best ways to help children to keep themselves safe while engaging in vigorous physical play is to role-model good ways of doing it, just as we would with any other area of learning. We can add to their knowledge and experience of keeping safe, either verbally or through our own bodies by way of demonstration or physical support. Role-model safe ways to fall, and talk through your own thoughts and emotions when engaging in exciting physical experiences.

Getting involved with children's physical play might involve leading, coaching or demonstrating a skill, being a playmate or even providing the other body to tumble with! This is particularly important with babies and very young children, when a 'tuned-in' adult is best placed to be able to gauge energy and pleasure levels from their contact with the child as they play physical games.

(Adapted from Daly and O'Connor 2009)

HAVE A THINK ABOUT... ROUGH AND TUMBLE PLAY

Did you like rough and tumble as a child? What do you think might be the reasons for this pleasure (or otherwise)?

What are the challenges in promoting and maintaining this kind of play in your setting?

How comfortable are you in getting involved yourself in this kind of activity with the children?

Do you think boys and girls have different experiences of rough and tumble?

How would you support a child who found this kind of play uncomfortable or threatening?

What help would you need to raise the profile of vigorous contact play in your setting?

Importance of play

Play is very important to physical development – and the body figures largely in a child's ability to play. Patricia Maude describes play as 'learning with the body' (Maude 2001:27) as it involves both gross and fine motor and muscle development as well as perceptual motor development. Much has been written about the importance of play for intellectual, social and emotional development, but the role of play in physical development (and vice versa) seems to be something that we take for granted, rather in the way that physical development itself has been taken for granted as something that just happens. It seems inevitable that children move when they play, whether they are running around vigorously outdoors or playing with buttons and beads or bricks and cuddly toys. Movement of one kind or another is always involved when children playfully interact, not just with their environment and the things in it, but also with the bodies of other people, as well as their own. Play experiences provide countless opportunities for children to spontaneously rehearse, practise and refine physical skills and to explore what their bodies can – and sometimes can't – do yet. As babies and young children acquire fundamental motor skills through their early play, they are then able to play increasingly more complex games, which in turn help them develop higher order physical, cognitive, social and emotional skills, abilities and dispositions. But if we believe that children are instinctively primed to move in order to develop not just their motor skills but also their sensory system, nerve networks and higher order brain structure, then clearly their spontaneous urge to play is also perhaps inextricably linked with this. Structured PE sessions with young children have a small part to play, providing they are brief, tailored to developmental need and, most importantly, fun – but they are not 'play'. It is spontaneous bursts of vigorous activity, followed by self-initiated rest and recovery, that seem to be the most valuable in developing neural networks. Key to this are linked indoor and outdoor spaces that children can move freely between and that provide the motivation and stimulus for spontaneous movement of all kinds, supported by interested and attentive adults.

In and out

Much has been written about the value of outdoor space for children's development and learning. Wanting to be able to connect with the weather and the natural environment, and to engage in activities that can't take place indoors so easily or effectively (digging up worms, splashing in puddles, rolling down hills etc.), has meant that most settings continue to place great emphasis on their outdoor provision and appreciate the value of the time children spend outdoors, often in all weathers. This is despite the downgrading of outdoor space in the revised EYFS (2012) as something desirable rather than essential. Physical development in particular is seen as an area of learning that has much to gain from outdoor activity, whether through traditional sports and PE sessions or in general outdoor play experiences. Movement play specialists, Jabadao, suggest that it is worth remembering that providing an indoor space for movement as part of continuous provision can also be very beneficial, particularly if you have concerns about children's motor skill development. It is easy to do with a couple of PE mats, alongside a wall or in a corner, and settings that experiment with this generally find that it soon becomes an essential part of continuous provision and that concerns about rowdiness and accidents are unfounded. What they see instead are children using the space for a variety of movement activities (including dance as well as rough and tumble) that encourage crawling and tummy play and support proprioception, vestibular development and the inhibition of reflexes.

Flow

One of the characteristics of play as described by Tina Bruce is the ability to be able to 'wallow' in experience (Bruce 2010:287). Although not exclusively a physical activity, there is no denying the sublime pleasure of a play experience that allows whole body 'wallowing'! In a similar vein, Mihaly Czikszentmihalyi (1997) writes about the importance of 'flow' for creativity and the completion of tasks (as well as for general happiness and contentment). For a person to be in a state of 'flow' whilst engaged in any activity, he believes that, among other characteristics, action, challenge and skill should be involved, that there should be no fear of failure and that reward should be for its own sake and not applied (or removed) as an external motivator (Czikszentmihalyi 1997, cited in Pound 2013:78). This has much to tell us about the implications of the way many of our so-called 'purposeful' learning activities for children are designed.

Never still?

Three-year-olds are believed to have the highest spontaneous activity levels of any age in the human life span (Maude 2001:37), being almost constantly on the move, even in their sleep! Unless, of course, their movement is restricted by being over-contained in seats, chairs and buggies and their motivation dimmed by too much screen time and negative reactions to their liveliness. Watching young children playing even with a sedentary activity, we are likely to see them shift and change position frequently. This is because their muscles contain a greater percentage of water than ours, and so they tire more easily. So in the course of a game in which they never lose concentration, children will sit and stand, kneel and crouch, shifting and changing their position whilst happily continuing to play. Patricia Maude describes how 'this natural and seemingly constant shifting satisfies the need to provide renewed stimulation to the muscles and to avoid muscle fatigue' (Maude 2001:18) and comments on how this fact is often lost on curriculum developers who continue to target the ability to sit still as a suitable learning goal for young children.

Sitting still?

Children only gradually gain control of their body and it is believed that the vestibular system, for example, isn't fully developed until at least seven years of age (Goddard Blythe 2004:17). Sally Goddard Blythe points out that being able to be still depends on mature motor skills. If being still involves balance, then it will be very hard to hold the body still until its balance mechanism (the vestibular system) is fully developed. Yet there is an expectation that very young children should learn to sit still as early as possible and that the way to make them learn this feat of body control is by demanding they sit still, long before their body is capable of it. Remembering that the vestibular system can *only* be developed by lots of movement and that young muscles need to shift when they are tired, it would seem that for a child's body to mature enough to be still, they actually need more movement and not less! As LeVoguer and Pasch clearly state,

> This has implications for provision and practice in early childhood settings and the first years of school. It is important to note that children cannot learn to be still through being still; fast and excitable movement precedes this ability to be still.
>
> (LeVoguer and Pasch 2014:101)

HAVE A THINK ABOUT... OUR EXPECTATIONS OF CHILDREN SITTING STILL

We've all done it. Sat there waiting for children to be still before we began a story, encouraged sitting on their bottoms and crossing their legs etc. ... and chided children whose fidgeting was a distraction.

What strategies are available to you to support and honour children's natural urge for movement?

What changes might you make to simplify the demands made on young children to be still, before they have the physical maturity to be able to do so?

Assessing physical development

There is currently very little official guidance available to support practitioners in their assessment of children's physical development, and what there is lacks depth and any acknowledgement of primitive reflexes and sensory integration. Let's look at what some of the key contributors to this field have to say about assessing physical development.

Sally Goddard Blythe – INPP

In an article based on a verbal presentation given to the Quality of Childhood Group in the European Parliament in 2011, Sally Goddard Blythe stated that, 'targets set by the EYFS tended to focus on *performance outcomes* rather than assessing and nurturing children's *Physical "readiness"* for formal education' (Goddard Blythe 2012a). Citing research across three countries, showing that many children did not have the motor skills that would enable them to 'perform well in an educational environment' (Goddard Blythe 2012a), she comments on the fact that assessment of growth and physical development has been largely ignored by education since routine developmental tests (carried out by doctors prior to starting school) were phased out in the 1980s. She suggests that assessment of primitive reflexes, postural reactions, balance and co-ordination would help us better understand children's developmental needs, particularly when they start school, and would enable the right form of treatment or remediation to address any issues and improve the child's 'readiness' to progress well. INPP provides training programmes for schools and practitioners, which include developmental screening tests (Goddard Blythe 2012b).

Penny Greenland – Jabadao

In her book *Hopping Home Backwards*, Penny Greenland (2000) provides helpful ideas for observing children in their movement play in order to assess areas of physical development that may need attention. The book includes simple charts that enable the practitioner to gauge and map aspects such as 'embodiment', 'what is happening', 'what isn't happening' and 'what is trying to happen', with ideas and suggestions for movement play activities to support areas of development.

Gill Connell and Cheryl McCarthy – Moving Smart

Moving Smart was founded in 1997 in New Zealand by Gill Connell, to help teachers and parents better understand the role movement plays in early childhood development. Her publication *A Moving Child is a Learning Child* (2014), co-authored with Cheryl McCarthy, introduces the 'The Kinetic Scale'™. Although not strictly an assessment tool (and definitely not a checklist), the scale provides a guide for integrating movement into a holistic learning environment, highlighting six physicalities – the senses, balance, intuition, power, coordination and control. With observation at the heart of the approach, they also offer a 'Movement Can-Do Guide' allowing practitioners to assess a child's current capabilities and select 'Smart Steps' activities suitable for developmental progress. They state very clearly that the guide is not meant for comparing children of the same age, nor should it be used 'to gauge where a child should be in her development. She is where she is. Start from there' (Connell and McCarthy 2014: 262).

Starting with the child

In this current climate of constant educational testing (and a new baseline assessment introduced for children entering reception class) it can be difficult for early years practitioners to hang on to their principles and resist pressure to be continuously assessing and comparing children against some flawed sense of what is considered average or 'normal' development, and pushing them to be 'above average' sooner and earlier. Development in any of the Prime areas is very much dependent on a child's *experience* – and is also contingent on that experience coming at the right time for their individual growth. Starting with the child means just that. Where they 'are' is where they need to be, for whatever reason. Through careful observation and attunement, a child's key people (one or two practitioners with whom the child has a special relationship and feels comfortable, safe and relaxed) are well placed to make assessments of a child's physical development, in consultation with the child's parents/carers. With this knowledge, matched with a good understanding of child development, they can plan to enrich and enhance the child's environment with experiences that will move them to the next stage, whilst also allowing them time for consolidation and to revisit earlier stages when needed. Rather than talking blithely about having high expectations of children, we ought perhaps to look at it from a slightly different angle. First, find the place where the child and your expectations *meet* – and then you can raise your expectations. This is particularly relevant when we think that many of our children are arriving in settings and schools, not yet ready for the expectations we might have of them, particularly if their early experiences have indicated a degree of vulnerability or, conversely, pressure to succeed at an early age. Tuning into their stage of physical development needs to become an important part of our initial and ongoing assessment of a child's progress so that we can spot any gaps (Greenland 2000) and provide the kinds of movement and sensory experiences that will make a difference – and continue to build their brains and nervous system.

Partnership with parents

Make a photographic display to share with parents the role of physical development and movement play across the EYFS areas of learning. Duplicate the photos to create a book or photo album that will still be around when the display needs replacing. Use it to reassure parents (and others) who may not appreciate the important motor skills development that needs to take place if children are to be truly 'ready' for school and further learning across the curriculum.

Partnership with professionals

■ Consider ways you can best support other professionals and those working with older children and families to understand the very particular nature of the EYFS as a stage in its own right – and not merely as preparation for later stages.

■ Support staff who are working with children in KS1 and 2 to appreciate the importance of physical development and movement play with regards to later learning, particularly in literacy and numeracy, and the value of continued physical activity and movement experiences beyond the EYFS.

Summary

This chapter looks at the EYFS through the lens of physical development, considering the important role played by sensory and motor skill development across all areas of learning and ways to ensure a rich environment that enables children to learn *through* movement as well as learning *about* movement.

The importance of play and assessment are considered, together with attitudes towards risk and challenge and ways to support robust vigorous play.

Implications for practice

■ We need to appreciate and maximise the cross-curricular opportunities for movement play, as well as emphasising the ways that physical experience informs learning.

■ An enriched physical environment includes not just the space and the resources, but also the positive attitudes of practitioners who honour and advocate for children's physical experience.

■ Practitioners who are confident in their understanding of child development and physical literacy are more readily able to offer children challenging environments that, in turn, build children's confidence and their physical skills as well as their resilience.

■ Consider how you increase and improve the quality of your assessments to include a more comprehensive perspective on physical literacy and its development, and how this will inform your practice.

■ A commitment is required to educational approaches that value a holistic view of the child that doesn't separate the body from the mind.

Playful ideas

Try these activities to spontaneously encourage dance and creativity, wherever you are... Although some ideas may seem age-specific, they can also be adapted to suit children at most stages of development within the EYFS and even beyond. Use them spontaneously, responding 'in the moment' to what your observations tell you about a child's developmental readiness, as well as in short bursts of structured activity in small groups, if and when appropriate.

Dancing hands

Start sitting down to explore the different dances your hands can do. Clapping, shaking, wriggling, crawling like spiders, tickling, slapping the floor, stretching to different places, patting different body parts, try movements up high, down low and to the sides. How about when your hands meet someone else's hands? What kind of dances can you do together? Clapping, shaking, squeezing, stroking, creepy crawly fingers, stretching together, patting each other, see saws, waving, hiding and appearing. What can your hands do today?

Dancing feet

Sitting down, explore all the different movements that your feet can do. Wriggling, stretching, circles, slapping on the floor, stretching to different places in the room, touching different parts of your body. What about upside down? Wriggling your feet high in the air as you fall back, turning upside down to reach your feet to the ceiling. Standing up you can explore stomping, marching, jumping, twisting, hopping, balancing, kicking, skipping. What can your feet do today?

Dancing scarves

Provide coloured fabric scarves and try these moves out. Music is not required but can add to the experience. Use any that inspires you, but plan for a range of styles and tempos including world, classical and pop music as well as children's music and songs. Use the music to inspire style and pace of scarf /dance action – from slow to fast, steady and marching, gentle and flowing, staccato (where the movements are sharply disconnected from each other) or syncopated (urgent and jerky).

- Dance with one scarf, or have one in each hand.
- If using one, sometimes swap and dance with it in your less dominant hand.
- Remember to make small movements with the scarves as well as large ones.
- Wiggle, shake and ripple the scarves.
- Wave or dance with them high up or low down to the floor.
- Hang them down from the hand in a pincer grip and twizzle the end on the floor.
- Move, stop, then move again.
- Make circles, triangles, squares in the air.
- Throw scarves up high and catch them, or let them drop to the floor.
- Spin and twirl with scarf, on the spot or travelling around the space.
- Run with scarf trailing behind or flying up high.
- Stand still and let your eyes focus on the scarf, following it as it moves around.
- Flick the scarf out from the body at all angles and in all directions.
- Make scarves ripple between two people.

- Sit child on the end of a scarf and slide them around.

- Imagine 'painting' the space with your scarves.

- Use the scarves to create a pattern or picture on the ground, then 'dissolve' the picture by 'sweeping' it up with hands or bare feet.

- Join in yourself, or stand back and observe free movements and creative ideas from the children.

All of these activities can help with integrating some reflexes and can support creative expression and thinking, as well as actively preparing brains and bodies for later reading and writing. Get moving and keep dancing!

Conclusion

Worldview

In an article entitled 'Worlds Apart' (2015a) Dr Lala Manners considers how physical activity in the early years is viewed across the world. Asking the same questions of practitioners in countries such as Finland, UEA, China and South Africa, she builds up a picture of responses that in some ways are very similar and in others very diverse. She notes that these perceptions of children (and their physicality) have wide implications for government policies and responses to young children and their families. 'Environment, transport, housing, education and welfare initiatives will be affected directly by the priorities established by agencies engaged and involved with young children's physical health and well-being.' Of course, priorities differ – in some parts of the world, nutrition and medical care are a priority and in war-affected areas physical and emotional safety must take precedence. This makes the obsession with obesity and sedentary activity in the 'minority' world (i.e. affluent countries where fewer people live) seem rather secondary. Despite this, there is genuine concern in the UK and other parts of the world that obesity is becoming more of a health risk among the poor than the wealthy, because of the impact of more readily available, cheaper foods that are highly processed and high in sugars – and sadly that our children are just not *moving* enough.

Health or education?

Dr Manners also points out the difference in perceptions across the world as to whether physical activity is seen as a health or an education issue. For those of us steeped in a holistic early years viewpoint, sustained by a belief that we are educating *and* caring for the 'whole child', whose wellbeing cannot be neatly boxed up into categories, this seems less of an issue. What is a continuing concern for us, however, is that much of the rhetoric around children's physical activity seems to keep missing a significant point. Children's bodies (and their physical development) are intrinsically linked to their brains and, therefore, physical activity and movement play are fundamental to brain development and children's learning potential. Whilst we continue to hear concerns about children's 'readiness' for school, their disruptive behaviour and poor levels of concentration and academic achievement, despite any number of 'booster' and remedial programmes, perhaps we need to pay more attention to children's early physical experiences in our attempts to 'close the gap' between children who appear to achieve and those who don't. Equally, a heavy emphasis on adult driven, scheduled physical activity in order to increase skills and improve the health of the nation's children isn't the only answer. Without an abundance of opportunities for spontaneous movement we are actively limiting brain development – and thus affecting the learning potential of our children as well as their physical and emotional wellbeing.

Motivation for spontaneous play

However, we have to face the sad fact that it isn't just a case of removing barriers to spontaneous movement, in order for children to engage in all the instinctive play that they need for their neurophysiological development. We now have young children who, for a variety of reasons, no longer have the same levels of motivation for spontaneous movement play as they might once have had. Many of them have spent their early lives being propped up and strapped into 'containers' that restrict their natural movements. They are no longer encouraged to play out or wander far from home with friends. Their playgrounds are covered with safety surfaces and mostly filled with unimaginative structures that don't encourage creativity or risk taking. Their homes are filled with technology that induces them to spend many hours in sedentary activity focusing on screens, with their thumbs and fingers getting more exercise than any other part of their body. Their after-school hours are filled with homework and extracurricular activities that, even when they are movement related, rarely involve doing something just for the fun of it. This may sound extreme, and it obviously isn't the case for all children, but it is more common than we would wish. So our children need us to actively provide the space, the opportunity and the provocation that will encourage them to run and climb, to swing and slide, to build dens and challenge themselves, just like generations of children have done before them.

Indoor movement

Although the outdoors is an important outlet for movement activity, the indoors also has much to offer. We encourage practitioners attending our Primed for Life training sessions to experiment with creating indoor movement areas, as suggested by movement play specialists, Jabadao. Those who do, report benefits far beyond the development of motor skills, commenting on the increased connection they feel when engaging with children in the movement corner. Rolling on the floor, dancing and crawling about with the children in this special space has had a powerful and positive impact on relationships, helping practitioners tune into children emotionally as well as physically. We also hear that for some children it is always the place they go to first on arrival at the setting, as if knowing that they need immediate physical activity. This provides evidence, should we need it, that the predictability and consistency of the area being part of continuous provision is very important to them. Over time, we may also begin to hear more about the kinds of increased cognitive capability that studies from around the world suggest are resulting from targeted work on children's retained reflexes, delayed motor skills and sensory processing issues (e.g. INPP 2011).

Fears that an indoor movement area may be disruptive or encourage unruly behaviour seem to be unfounded. Indeed, the opposite has been noted, with practitioners reporting a reduction in behavioural issues in general, and amazement at how sensibly the children tend to use the space. Helping other colleagues and parents to understand the purposes of an indoor movement area is key to its success, however, because for many it seems it is still a step too far!

Shifting attitudes

This is our main reason in wanting to write this book – to help shift attitudes towards physical activity and movement play in our early years settings. Young children are not meant to spend their days sitting still – or even sitting and fidgeting! But pressure from governments to 'schoolify' care in early childhood is inevitably leading to reduced levels of physical activity and less time for spontaneous movement and sensory-rich play. As practitioners we need to challenge this pressure, with evidence from our own observations of children and our knowledge of child development. In 2014 a major study in response to increased provision for two-year-olds found that,

> Despite widespread recognition of the importance of outdoor play in the early years literature and in the key informant interviews and case study settings, fewer online survey respondents selected movement and physical development – the third prime area of the EYFS – as one of their three key dimensions of quality. This may indicate a need for further efforts to raise awareness of the importance of movement and physical development.
>
> (Georgeson et al. 2014)

Clearly there is still some work to be done to change the mindset that suggests physical development isn't really that important (in comparison to communication and language, for example). However, a shift in attitude and belief can only come with increased awareness, knowledge and understanding, and that involves training and continuing professional development (CPD). We have witnessed firsthand the changes that can take place when practitioners are exposed to wider understandings of physical development and develop an appreciation of the links between this crucial Prime area and *all* other areas of learning. The opportunity to step back into 'their own shoes as a child', exploring their early experiences of physical and sensory development and connecting with the sensations as well as the emotions, better enables them to 'step into the shoes' of the children with whom they work and to tune into their needs and starting points. Furthermore, once practitioners increase their knowledge and understanding of physical development, they begin to view the early years curriculum through a different lens, and become much better equipped to challenge ill-informed views and policies on the care and education of young children.

Lifelong movement play

We'd also like to see that shift happen in those who work with older children too – and, indeed, on into adulthood! We firmly believe that there is a place for intergenerational work with elders and young children, exploring what it means to 'feel at home' in our bodies and acknowledging the contribution that movement and sensory experience make to our wellbeing at any age. We also believe that a raised awareness of the importance of movement and sensory processing in early childhood can support parents in raising confident, well-balanced children. This means sharing that information with older children and teenagers too, so that they are better equipped to take care of their own bodies, as well as any future children they may have.

Assessment for the future

As we write, there are plans in England for new Baseline Assessments to come into place in the Reception year. The approved commercial assessments vary widely in quality and there is little, if any, emphasis on physical development, unlike the medical checks that once took place as a child entered compulsory schooling. Given the increasing evidence that the retention of early reflexes and the development of motor skills may play a considerable part in a child's 'readiness for school', it seems that a physical screening might be more useful in determining the developmental needs of children at this age. This would provide Reception class staff with valuable information, enabling them to target appropriate physical experiences to address reflex inhibition and motor skill development. This would increase the likelihood of each child being able to fully access their education.

Movement, wellbeing and touch

Equally important in our understanding of the 'gaps' that might exist in children's early development is an appreciation of the crucial nature of touch in the lives of the young children with whom we work. 'Touch is a key means of communication for young children and as such a vital aspect of pedagogy' (Pound 2013:44). To many of us it seems unimaginable that a child would spend their earliest years not knowing the warm and loving touch of family and carers, but for a variety of reasons that seems to increasingly be the case. It is easy enough to see the emotional damage this may cause, perhaps, as the link between warm, affectionate touch and secure attachments is without dispute. But, just as early movement experiences have an important contribution to make to the development of neural pathways and future learning, so too does security of attachment and the sensory stimulus that accompanies it. Sadly, we won't solve the nation's educational problems simply with a curriculum of 'hugs', but LeVoguer and Pasch reinforce the significance of the links between the two in their statement that, 'early childhood practice needs to understand and acknowledge the primacy of movement and touch for children's well-being and to consider that there are very real risks to children's emotional, social and cognitive development if movement and touch are disregarded' (LeVoguer and Pasch 2014:105).

Primed for life

This is particularly challenging when we consider the current climate of austerity and global uncertainty, and the impact this is likely to have on the resilience and wellbeing of our most vulnerable children. Now more than ever, we need to be raising strong, healthy, well-balanced children, capable of handling whatever life will throw at them in the future. Let's not forget, our body-based resources all come for free – and could provide us with everything we need in order to keep going when things get tough. However, unless we broaden our attention to the *whole* child – and not just the bit on top of their shoulders – we will be raising disembodied children. Children may find their instinctive biological drive for movement overruled by adults, teachers, learning environments, programmes and policies, actively missing out on the key fundamental developments for mind and body that can prime them for life.

More information

Websites

www.primedforlife.co.uk
www.jabadao.org
www.neurologicalreorganization.org
www.inpp.org.uk
www.movingsmart.co.nz
www.rhythmicmovement.co.uk
www.spdfoundation.net
www.retainedneonatalreflexes.com.au
www.ludusdance.org
www.feldenkrais.co.uk
www.countthekicks.org.uk
www.nct.org.uk/parenting/baby-massage
www.parentingworx.co.nz
www.theknowingbodynetwork.co.uk
www.watchingdance.org
www.sirenfilms.com
www.savechildhood.net
www.dyspraxiafoundation.org.uk

Video and films

Siren Films – www.sirenfilms.co.uk
The Power of Physical Play
All About the Outdoors
Jabadao Films – info@jabado.org
Developmental Movement Play
A Missing Piece of the Jigsaw

Pikler Institute Films – www.pickler.hu
Freedom to Move on One's Own
Feldenkrais – Rolling
http://www.youtube.com/watch?v=D9Ko7U1pLlg
Lactancia Materna – breastfeeding
https://www.youtube.com/watch?v=0JNdwZ1TU0USalud CZ8/Youtube

Resources to support physical development and dance in the early years

www.sensory-processing-disorder.com
www.specialneedstoys.com
www.chewigem.co.uk – chewy 'jewellery'
www.primedforlife.co.uk – Dancing Scarves

Further reading

Brownlee, F., & Norris, L. (2015) *Promoting Attachment with a Wiggle, Giggle, Hug and Tickle.* London: Jessica Kingsley.

Daly, A. *Body Doodles* (Resource Pack). Available from www.earlyarts.co.uk.

Daly, A./Ludus Dance (2009) *Reaching for More: Project Evaluation.* Available from http://www.dancewell.org.uk/#!early-years.

Goddard Blythe, S. (2012) *Assessing Neuromotor Readiness for Learning: The INPP Developmental Screening Test and School Intervention Programme.* Chester: Wiley Blackwell.

Mountstephen, M. (2011) *How to Detect Developmental Delay and What to do Next: Practical Interventions for Home and School.* London: Jessica Kingsley.

White, J. (2015) *Every Child a Mover: A Practical Guide to Providing Young Children with the Physical Opportunities They Need.* London: Early Education.

White, J. *Making a Mud Kitchen.* Available from: http://www.muddyfaces.co.uk/mud_kitchens.php.

Glossary

amygdala the part of the brain that helps control our impulses

asymmetrical tonic neck reflex (ATNR) reflex response to the rotation of the head

atypical a different way of developing, which may – or may not – indicate or be symptomatic of an impairment or specific need

axon a long thread-like part of a nerve cell along which impulses are conducted from the cell body to other cells

Babinski reflex triggered by stroking the outside of the sole up to the little toe and across to the big toe, making the toes fan out and the big toe overextend. Also known as the extensor plantar response

Babkin reflex when quick pressure is applied to the palms, the baby's mouth opens and the head turns. Also known as the palmar-mandibular reflex

bilaterality mirrored movements where one side of the body does the same as the other side

central nervous system (CNS) consists of the brain and the spinal cord

cephalocaudal development 'top-down' development from head to toe

corpus callosum a band of nerve fibres that join the two sides of the brain

corticospinal tract very long axons that originate in the brain at the cerebral cortex and then cross over at the top of the cervical spine (neck) before they travel down each side of the spinal cord. Also known as the 'pyramidal' tract

cross-lateral using the arms or legs to cross over the midlines

dendrite a short, branched extension of a nerve cell, along which impulses received from other cells are transmitted to the cell body

dyspraxia a form of developmental coordination disorder (DCD) affecting fine and/or gross motor coordination in children and adults. It may also affect speech. It is distinct from other motor disorders such as cerebral palsy and stroke, and occurs across the range of intellectual abilities. Individuals may vary in how their difficulties present: these may change over time depending on environmental demands and life experiences

extension the state of being extended, stretched out or lengthened, particularly in this case in relation to a limb or joints

extensor muscle a contracting muscle that supports lifting and extension of a limb

fine motor control the coordination of muscles, bones and nerves to produce small, precise movements

flexion bending or being bent, especially in a limb or joint

flexor muscle a contracting muscle that supports a limb or part of the body to bend

gross motor control control of the large muscle groups of the body e.g. those in the arms, legs and core

hippocampus part of the brain involved in forming, storing and processing memory

homolaterality to be able to move one part of the body whilst keeping the other parts still

homologous movements where body parts make the same movements

laterality where one part of the body can do something in the opposite way to another part

locomotion the ability to move from one place to another

midlines three invisible lines dividing the body up into sectors from left to right, from front to back and from top to bottom

Moro reflex (the startle response) involves the arms opening out and extending and a sudden intake of breath. Can be activated by a range of sudden or unexpected sensory experiences

motor neurons control voluntary movement by transmitting messages in the form of electrical impulses from the brain or spinal cord to the muscles

myelination a process that insulates the nerves with a fatty layer called myelin, and helps create strong neural pathways

nervous system runs throughout the body and is made up of the brain, the spinal cord and peripheral nerves. The brain is the 'head quarters' of the nervous system

neuron a nerve cell that receives and sends electrical signals over long distances within the body

neurophysiological development used by some specialists to describe the interdependent nature of body and brain development, including the integration of the senses and the development of a fully functioning nervous system

neurotransmitters chemical messengers that transmit information from a nerve cell to another nerve, muscle, organ, etc.

ontogenetic behaviours that are influenced by learning and the environment

palmar grasp reflex putting a finger in a newborn's hand triggers the fingers to close in a palmar grasp

peripheral nervous system (PNS) is made up of all the nerve fibres branching off from the spinal cord and extending to all parts of the body including the neck and limbs, torso, muscles and internal organs

phylogenetic behaviours emerging naturally as the child matures

plantar reflex triggered by stroking the sole of the foot on the outer side, resulting in flexion. Similar to the palmar grasp reflex

positional plagiocephaly flat spots on the head

postural reflexes responses that control the posture of the body and limbs

praxis in movement, the neurological process of planning what to do and then doing it

prone lying on the tummy, face downwards

proprioception the unconscious perception of movement and spatial orientation arising from sensations within the body itself so that we know where our bodies start and finish and where we are in relation to the rest of the world

proximo-distal development describes the process of movement control emerging and extending from the 'proximal' (close to the body) out to the 'distal' (furthest from the centre of the body)

reflex an involuntary action or response

rooting reflex assists in breast feeding as the baby automatically turns the face toward a stimulus and makes rooting motions with the mouth when the cheek or lip is touched

sensory neurons send messages to the brain from incoming messages from the senses

sensory processing the brain's ability to organise and process information received from the environment through the senses. Also referred to as sensory integration

spinal galant reflex exists in the womb. Sensitive spots on the back cause the baby to 'squirm' and arch the body one way and then the other as they touch the walls of the womb and birth canal, assisting in delivery

supine lying on the back, face upwards

symmetric tonic neck reflex (STNR) if the arms are stretched, then the legs will remain bent and vice versa

tonic labyrinthine reflex (TLR) aligning reflex responding directly to the position of the head

torticollis distortion of the neck due to restricted movement

'typical' describes the characteristics seen in most children's development within a fairly loose framework or range

vestibular system the sensory mechanism in the inner ear that detects movement of the head and helps to control balance

Bibliography

Adolph, K. (2002) Learning to Keep Balance. In Kail, R. (ed.) *Advances in Child Development and Behaviour* (Vol. 30). New York: Elsevier.

Adolph, K.E., Karasik, L.B., & Tamis-LeMonda, C.S. (2009) Moving Between Cultures: Cross-Cultural Research on Motor Development. In Bornstein, M.H. (ed.) *Handbook of Cross-cultural Developmental Science, Vol 1: Domains of Development Across Cultures* [Online]. Available at http://jakestone.net/wikipics/pdfs/CultureChapter.pdf [Accessed 26 November 2015].

Ahn, R.R., Miller, L.J., Milberger, S., & McIntosh, D.N. (2004) Prevalence of Parents' Perceptions of Sensory Processing Disorders among Kindergarten Children. *American Journal of Occupational Therapy* [Online] 58, 287–293. Available from: http://www.spdfoundation.net/files/9614/2430/1228/ahn_miller.pdf [Accessed 23 August 2015].

Archer, C. & Siraj, I. (2015) *Encouraging Physical Development through Movement Play*. London: Sage.

Ardiel, E.L., & Rankin, C.H. (2010) The Importance of Touch in Development. *Paediatrics & Child Health* 15(3), 153–156. Available from: http://www.ncbi.nlm.nih.gov/pmc/articles/PMC2865952/ [Accessed 20 July 2015].

Ayres, A.J. (1972) *Sensory Integration and Learning Disorders*. Los Angeles: Western Psychological Services (cited in Hannaford 2005:44–48).

Ayres, A.J. (2005) *Sensory Integration and the Child: 25th Anniversary Edition*. Los Angeles: Western Psychological Services.

Barsch, R.H. (1968) Achieving Perceptual-motor Efficiency. A Self-orientated Approach to Learning. *Perceptual-Motor Curriculum* (Vol. 1). Seattle: Special Child Publications.

Baum, V. (1888–1960) [Online quote] Available at: http://thinkexist.com/quotes/like/there_are_shortcuts_to_happiness-and_dancing_is/339637/4.html [Accessed 7 September 2015].

Bayley, R., & Featherstone, S. (2009) *The Cleverness of Boys*. London: A&C Black Publishers Ltd.

Bein-Weirzbinski, W. (2001) Persistent Primitive Reflexes in Elementary School Children, Effect on Oculomotor and Visual Perception. Paper presented at the *13th European Conference of Neurodevelopmental Delay in Children with Specific Learning Difficulties*, Chester, UK.

Ben-Sasson, A., Carter, A.S., & Briggs Gowan, M.J. (2009) Sensory Over-responsivity in Elementary School: Prevalence and Social-emotional Correlates. *Journal of Abnormal Child Psychology* [Online] 37, 705–716. Available from: http://spdfoundation.net/files/5414/2430/1236/CARTER1.PDF [Accessed 23 August 2015].

Berrol, C.F. (2006) *Neuroscience Meets Dance/Movement Therapy: Mirror Neurons, the Therapeutic Process and Empathy* [Online]. Available from: http://www.sciencedirect.com/science/article/pii/S0197455606000438 [Accessed 24 August 2015].

Bertram, T., & Pascal, C. (2002) What Counts in Early Learning. In Saracho, O.N. & Spodek, B. (eds.) *Contemporary Perspectives in Early Childhood Curriculum*, pp. 241–256. Greenwich, CT: Information Age.

Biel, L., & Peske, N. (2009) *Raising a Sensory Smart Child.* New York: Penguin.

Bilton, H. (2002) *Outdoor Play in the Early Years: Management and Innovation* (2nd edn.). Abingdon: David Fulton.

Biswas-Diener, R. (2015) *The Brain and Nervous System* [Online]. Available from: http://nobaproject.com/modules/the-brain-and-nervous-system [Accessed 9 August 2015].

Blomberg, H. (2011) *Movements that Heal.* Queensland: BookPal.

Boorman, P. (1988) The Contributions of Physical Activity to Development in the Early Years. In Blenkin, G.M. & Kelly, A.V. (eds.) *Early Childhood Education. A Developmental Curriculum*, pp. 231–250. London: Paul Chapman Publishing.

Bowlby, J. (1988) *A Secure Base.* Abingdon: Routledge.

Bresler. L. (ed.) (2004) *Knowing Bodies, Moving Minds: Towards Embodied Teaching and Learning.* Dordrecht: Kluwer Academic Publishers.

Brodal, P. (1998) *The Central Nervous System: Structure and Function.* Oxford: Oxford University Press.

Bruce, T. (2010) Play, the Universe and Everything! In Moyles, J. (ed.) *The Excellence of Play* (3rd edn.), pp.277–288. Maidenhead: Open University Press.

Capute, A.J. et al. (1981) Primitive Reflexes: A Factor in Non-verbal Language in Early Infancy. In Stark, R. (ed.) *Language Behaviour in Infancy and Early Childhood.* New York: Elsevier.

Carlson, M., Earls, F., & Todd, R.D. (1988) The Importance of Regressive in the Development of the Nervous System: Towards a Neurological Biological Theory of Child Development. *Psychological Development* 6(1), 1–22 (cited in Macintyre 2009).

Clopton, H. (2013) *Crawling and Creeping ... a Milestone that Should Never be Missed!* [Online]. Available from: https://pediatrictherapist.wordpress.com/2013/01/18/crawling-and-creeping-a-milestone-that-should-never-be-missed/ [Accessed 7 September 2015].

Connell, G. (2015) personal communication.

Connell, G., & McCarthy, C. (2014) *A Moving Child is a Learning Child: How the Body Teaches the Brain to Think.* Minneapolis: Free Spirit Publishing.

The Connexion (2015) *France Bans Wi-fi in Nurseries* [Online]. Available at: http://www.connexionfrance.com/france-wifi-schools-ban-children-six-nurseries-daycare-kindergartens-homes-electromagnetic-waves-16637-view-article.html [Accessed 24 August 2015].

Czikszentmihalyi, M. (1997) *Creativity, Flow and the Psychology of Discovery and Invention.* New York: Harper Perennial.

Daly, A., & O'Connor, A. (2009) Learning Development: Physical Development Parts 1–5. *Nursery World* [Online], March–July 2009. Available from: www.nurseryworld.co.uk [Accessed 28 August 2015].

Daly, A., & O'Connor, A. (2013) EYFS Best Practice: All About ... Dance in the Early Years. *Nursery World* [Online], 22 March 2013. Available from: www.nurseryworld.co.uk [Accessed 28 August 2015].

Da Ros-Voseles, D., & Fowler-Haughey, S. (2007) Why Children's Dispositions Should Matter to All Teachers. *Journal of the National Association for the Education of Young Children* [Online]. Available from: http://eclkc.ohs.acf.hhs.gov/hslc/tta-system/teaching/

eecd/Domains%20of%20Child%20Development/Science/WhyChildrensDi.htm [Accessed 13 August 2015].

Delacato, C. (1970) *The Diagnosis and Treatment of Speech and Reading Problems.* Springfield, IL: Charles C. Thomas.

Dempsey, M. (2013) *Rhythmic Movement Training International: Reflex Integration Chart Set.* USA & Australia: Rhythmic Training International.

Diamond, M. (1988) *Enriching Heredity: The Impact of the Environment on the Anatomy of the Brain.* New York: Free Press.

Doherty, J., & Brennan, P. (2008) *Physical Education and Development 3–11: A Guide for Teachers.* Abingdon: Routledge.

Duffy, B. (2004) EYFS Best Practice: All About ... Messy Play. *Nursery World* [Online], 3 November 2004. Available from: www.nurseryworld.co.uk [Accessed 29 August 2015].

Durie, B. (2005) Doors of Perception. *New Scientist* [Online]. Available from: www.newscientist.com [Accessed 29 August 2015].

The Dyspraxia Foundation (2015*) Dyspraxia at a Glance* [Online]. Available from: http://www.dyspraxiafoundation.org.uk/about-dyspraxia/dyspraxia-glance/ [Accessed 8 July 2015].

Early Education (2012) *Development Matters in the Early Years Foundation Stage (EYFS).* London: Early Education [Online]. Available from: http://www.foundationyears.org.uk/files/2012/03/Development-Matters-FINAL-PRINT-AMENDED.pdf [Accessed 13 August 2015].

Feldenkrais, M. (1980*) Body and Mind* (excerpts) [Online]. Available from http://feldenkrais-method.org/archive/feldenkrais-method/#intro [Accessed 31 August 2015].

Fiorentino, M.R. (1981) *A Basis for Sensori-motor Development – Normal and Abnormal.* Springfield, IL: Charles C. Thomas (cited in Goddard Blythe 2009:107).

Francis, D., & Meaney, M.J. (1999) Maternal Care and the Development of Stress Responses. *Neurobiology* (Current Opinion), 9, 128–134 (cited in Hannaford 2005:44–45).

Gallahue, D., & Ozmun, J. (1995) *Understanding Motor Development* (Third edn.) Madison, WI: Brown and Benchmark.

Gaunt, C. (2011) *Motor Skills Gap Hampers Young Children's Learning* [Online]. Available from: www.nurseryworld.co.uk [Accessed 13 August 2015].

Georgeson, J., Campbell-Barr, V., Mathers, S., Boag-Munroe, G., Parker-Rees, R., & Caruso, F. (2014) [Online] *Two-year-olds in England: An Exploratory Study.* Available from: http://tactyc.org.uk/research/ [Accessed 8 September 2009].

Gerber, M. (1998) *Basic Principles* [Online]. Available from: https://www.rie.org/educaring/ries-basic-principles/ [Accessed 6 July 2015].

Gerber, M. (2009) cited in *Emmi Pikler's Guiding Principles* [Online]. Available from: http://www.parentingworx.co.nz/fantastic-reading/emmi-piklers-8-guiding-principles/ [Accessed 23 August 2015].

Gill, T. (2007) *No Fear: Growing up in a Risk Averse Society* [Online]. Available from: https://timrgill.files.wordpress.com/2010/10/no-fear-19-12-07.pdf Calouste Gulbenkian Foundation London [Accessed 26 July 2015].

Giordano, G.G. (1953) *Acta Neurologica* (Neapel) Feb 1953, III. Quaderno, p.313 (cited in Goddard Blythe 2009).

Goddard Blythe, S. (2004) *The Well Balanced Child: Movement and Early Learning* (Revised edn.). Stroud: Hawthorn Press.

Goddard Blythe, S. (2005) *The Well Balanced Child: Movement and Early Learning* (Revised edn.). Stroud: Hawthorn Press.

Goddard Blythe, S. (2009) *Attention, Balance and Coordination: The ABC of Learning Success.* Chichester: John Wiley & Sons.

Goddard Blythe, S. (2012a) The Right to Move: Assessing Neuromotor Readiness for Learning – Why Physical Development in the Early Years Supports Educational Success. *Improving the Quality of Childhood in Europe 2012* (Volume 3) [Online]. Available from: www.allianceforchildhood.eu/book-improving-the-quality-of-childhood-in-europe-2012 [Accessed 5 August 2015].

Goddard Blythe, S. (2012b) *Assessing Neuromotor Readiness for Learning The INPP developmental screening test and school intervention programme.* Chester: Wiley Blackwell.

Greenfield, S. (1996) *The Human Mind Explained.* London: Cassell (cited in Pound 2013).

Greenland, P. (2000) *Hopping Home Backwards: Body Intelligence and Movement Play.* Leeds: Jabadao.

Griffin, P. (2011) *Neuro Motor Immaturity* [Online]. Available from: http://www.inpp.org.uk/wp-content/uploads/2012/11/Early-Years-and-NMD.pdf [Accessed 7 September 2015].

Gura, P. (1996) *Resources for Early Learning: Children, Adults and Stuff.* London: Hodder and Stoughton.

Hannaford, C. (2005) *Smart Moves: Why Learning Is Not All in Your Head* (2nd edn.). Salt Lake City: Great Ocean Publishers.

Harada, S., & Saito, T. (1997). *Ashi karano kenkou zukuri: Okaasan to kodomo no tameno kenkou zukuri.* Tokyo: Chuou Houki. (In Japanese) (cited in Walsh 2004).

INPP (2011) *Reports from a Few of the Hungarian Schools Following the INPP Programme* [Online]. Available from: http://www.inpp.org.uk/wp-content/uploads/2011/07/Reports-from-a-few-of-the-Hungarian-schools.pdf [Accessed 8 September 2015].

Jabadao (2009) *More of Me* [Online]. Available from: http://www.jabadao.org/storage/downloads/More_of_Me_Executive_Summary.pdf [Accessed: 13 August 2015].

Jarvis, P. (2013) The McMillan Sisters and the 'Deptford Welfare Experiment'. *Early Years TACTYC* [Online]. Available from: http://tactyc.org.uk [Accessed 9 August 2015].

Jess, M., & McIntyre, J. (2013) Move On. *Nursery World* [Online]. Available from: www.nurseryworld.co.uk 29 January [Accessed 29 August 2015].

Karmiloff -Smith, A. (1994) *Baby It's You.* London: Ebury Press.

Katz, L.G. (1993) Dispositions: Definitions and Implications for Early Childhood Practices. *Catalog No. 211 Perspectives from ERIC/EECE: Monograph Series no. 4* [Online]. Available from: http://ceep.crc.uiuc.edu/ eecearchive/books/disposit.html (cited in Da Ros-Voseles and Fowler-Haughey 2007).

Kaye, K. (1977) Toward the Origin of Dialogue. In Schaffer, H.R. (ed.) *Studies in Mother Infant Interaction.* London: Academic Press (cited in Goddard Blythe 2009).

Knost, L. (2013) *Two Thousand Kisses a Day: Gentle Parenting Through the Ages and Stages.* USA: Little Hearts Books.

Kranowitz, C.S. (2005) *The Out-of-Sync Child: Recognizing and Coping with Sensory Processing Disorder.* New York: Penguin.

Kranowitz, C.S. (2009) *The Vestibular System and Auditory-Language Processing* [Online]. Developmental Delay Resources Available from: http://devdelay.org/newsletter/articles/html/53-vestibular-system-auditory-language-processing.html [Accessed 6 July 2015].

Laevers, F., (Red.), (1994) *The Leuven Involvement Scale for Young Children.* Manual and video. Experiential Education Series, No 1. Leuven: Centre for Experiential Education. (44 pp). Available from: http://www.kindengezin.be/img/sics-ziko-manual.pdf [Accessed 26 November 2015].

Lawrence, R.A., & Lawrence, R.M. (2010) *Breastfeeding: A Guide for the Medical Profession.* Philadelphia: Elsevier – Health Sciences Division.

Levine, S. (1957) Infantile Experience and Resistance to Physiological Stress. *Science* 126, 405–406 (cited in Hannaford 2005:45).

LeVoguer, M., & Pasch, J. (2014) Physical Well-being: Autonomy, Exploration and Risk-taking. In Manning-Morton, J. (ed.) *Exploring Well-being in the Early Years*. Maidenhead: Open University Press.

Lindon, J. (2011) *Too Safe for Their Own Good* (2nd edn.). London: National Children's Bureau.

Macintyre, C. (2009) *Dyspraxia in the Early Years* (2nd edn.). Abingdon: David Fulton.

Manners, L. (2015a) Learning and Development: Physical Development – Worlds Apart *Nursery World* [Online]. Available from: www.nurseryworld.co.uk [Accessed 9 September 2015].

Manners, L. (2015b) PD: Principles into Practice. *Nursery World* [Online]. Available from: www.nurseryworld.co.uk (12–25 January) [Accessed 28 August 2015].

Masi,W.S., & Cohen Leiderman, R. (2004) *Baby Play*. San Francisco: Weldon Owen Inc.

Mast, F.W., Preuss, N., Hartmann, M., & Grabherr, L. Spatial Cognition, Body Representation and Affective Processes: The Role of Vestibular Information Beyond Ocular Reflexes and Control of Posture. *Frontiers in Integrative Science* [Online]. Available from: http://www.ncbi.nlm.nih.gov/pmc/articles/PMC4035009/ [Accessed 23 November 2015].

Maude, P. (2001) *Physical Children, Active Teaching: Investigating Physical Literacy*. Buckingham: OUP.

Meaney, M.J., Aitken, D.H., van Berkel, C., & Sapolsky, R.M. (1988) Effects of Neonatal Handling on Age Related Impairments Associated with the Hippocampus. *Science* 239, 776–768 (cited in Hannaford 2005:45).

Money, R. (2006) Introduction to: Pikler, E., & Pap, K. (2006) Unfolding of Infants' Natural Gross Motor Development. From the original publication *Terminology of basic Body Postures and Positions* (1978). Translated by Városy Tōth. Los Angeles: Resources for Infant Educators (RIE).

Mooney, C.G. (2013) *Theories of Childhood: An Introduction to Dewey, Montessori, Erikson, Piaget, and Vygotsky*. St. Paul: Redleaf Professional Library.

Morton, K. (2012) Links Shown between Neuromotor Skills and Academic Performance. *Nursery World* [Online]. Available from: www.nurseryworld.co.uk [Accessed 13 August 2015].

Moylett, H., & Stewart, N. (2012) *Understanding the Revised Early Years Foundation Stage*. London: Early Education.

NICHD (National Institute of Child Health and Development) (2014) *What are the Parts of the Nervous System?* [Online]. Available from: https://www.nichd.nih.gov/health/topics/neuro/conditioninfo/Pages/parts.aspx [Accessed 28 August 2005].

Nurse, A.D (2009) *Physical Development in the Early Years Foundation Stage*. Abingdon: Routledge.

O'Connor, A. (2010) Practice in Pictures: Mud Mud… [Online]. *Nursery World*, 2 December 2010. Available from: http://sirenfilms.co.uk/wp-content/uploads/2013/12/UCmessy playmud.pdf [Accessed 23 August 2015].

O'Connor, A. (2015) EYFS Best Practice: All About … Sensory Development. *Nursery World* [Online]. Available from: www.nurseryworld.co.uk [Accessed 28 August 2015].

O'Connor, A. (2014) *Health and Wellbeing*. London: Practical Pre-school Books.

Odent, M. (2002) The First Hour Following Birth: Don't Wake the Mother! *Midwifery Today* [Online]. Available at www.midwiferytoday.com/articles/firsthour.asp [Accessed 24 August 2015].

Page, J., Clare, A. & Nutbrown, C. (2013) *Working with Babies and Young Children: From Birth to Three* (2nd edn.). London: Sage.

Paley, V.G. (2004) *A Child's Work: The Importance of Fantasy Play*. London: University of Chicago Press.

Passmore, J. (1972) On Teaching to be Critical. In Dearden, R.F., Hirst, P.H., & Peters, R.S. (eds.) *Education and the Development of Reason*, pp. 415–433. London: Routledge & Kegan Paul.

Patterson, C. (2008) *Child Development*. New York: McGraw-Hill.

Pearce, J.C. (1986) *The Magical Child Matures*. New York: Bantam Books (cited in Hannaford 2005:46).

Pikler, E. (1971) Learning of Motor Skills on the Basis of Self-Induced Movements. In Hellmuth, J. (ed.) *Exceptional Infant, Vol 2: Studies in Abnormalities*. New York: Bruner/ Mazel, Inc.

Pikler, E., & Pap, K. (2006) Unfolding of Infants' Natural Gross Motor Development. From the publication *Terminology of Basic Body Postures and Positions* (1978). Translated by Városy Tóth. Los Angeles: Resources for Infant Educators (RIE).

Pinto, C. (2006) Foreword to: Pikler, E., & Pap, K. (2006) *Unfolding of Infants' Natural Gross Motor Development*. From the original publication *Terminology of Basic Body Postures and Positions* (1978). Translated by Városy Tóth. Los Angeles: Resources for Infant Educators (RIE).

Ponsonby, A.L., Smith, K., Williamson, E., Bridge, D., Carmichael, A., Dwyer, T., Jacobs, A., & Keeffe, J., (2013) *Poor Stereoacuity Among Children with Poor Literacy: Prevalence and Associated Factors* [Online]. Available from: http://www.ncbi.nlm.nih.gov/pubmed/ 23241825 [Accessed 14 August 2015].

Portwood, M. (2003) *Dyslexia and Physical Education*. Abingdon: David Fulton.

Pound, L. (2013) *Quick Guides for Early Years: Physical Development*. London: Hodder Education.

Radwan, K. (2009) *Sensory Attachment Integration* [Online]. Available from: http://www. sensoryattachmentintervention.com/Documents/Adoption%20UK%20Article.pdf [Accessed 23 August 2015].

RCOG (Royal College of Obstetricians and Gynaecologists) (2011) Reduced Fetal Movements. *Green–top Guideline No. 57* [Online]. Available from: https://www.rcog.org.uk/globalassets/ documents/guidelines/gtg_57.pdf [Accessed 7 September 2015].

Righard, L., & Alade, M.O. (1990) Effect of Delivery Room Routine on Success of First Breast Feed. *Lancet* 3/336(8723):1105–1107 (cited in Goddard Blythe 2009).

RMTI (Rhythmic Movement Training International) (2015) *Movements That Heal: Tonic Labyrinthine Reflex* [Online]. Available at http://www.rhythmicmovement.com/en/ primitive-reflexes/tonic-labyrinthine-reflex-tlr [Accessed on 24 August 2015].

RNR (Retained Neonatal Reflexes) (2015) *Reflexes Explained* [Online]. Available at http:// www.retainedneonatalreflexes.com.au/reflexes/tonic-labyrinthine-reflex/ [Accessed 24 August 2015].

Robinson, K. (2006) *Do Schools Kill Creativity?* Video recording TED [Online]. Available at http://www.ted.com/talks/ken_robinson_says_schools_kill_creativity?language=en [Accessed 11 August 2015].

Rovee-Collier, C. (1999) The Development of Infant Memory. *Current Directions in American Psychology* 8(3) [Online]. Available from: https://www.google.com/search?client=safari &rls=en&q=(Rovee-Collier+1999)&ie=UTF-8&oe=UTF-8 [Accessed 14 August 2015].

Rowe, N. (1994–5) Personal communication cited in Goddard Blythe, S. (2004) *The Well-Balanced Child*. Stroud: Hawthorn Press.

Sasse, M. (2002) *Tomorrow's Children for Parents!* Australia: Toddler Kindy GymbaROO.

Sensory Processing Disorder Foundation (2015) *Red Flags of Sensory Processing Disorder* [Online]. Available from: http://www.spdfoundation.net/about-sensory-processing-disorder/redsflags/ [Accessed 23 August 2015].

Sensory Processing Disorder Foundation (2015) *Research: Findings from the SPD Scientific Work Group* [Online]. Available from: http://www.spdfoundation.net/research/newresearch/ [Accessed 23 August 2015].

Sensory Processing Disorder Foundation (2015) *About SPD* [Online]. Available from: http://www.spdfoundation.net/about-sensory-processing-disorder/ [Accessed 23 August 2015].

Singhal, A. Morley, R., Cole, T., Kennedy, K., Sonksen, P., Isaacs, E., Fewtrell, M., Elias-Jones, A., Stephenson,T., & Lucas, A. (2007) Infant Nutrition and Stereoacuity at Age 4–6 Years. *American Journal of Clinical Nutrition* 12(1), 134 (cited in Goddard Blythe 2009:122).

Society for Neuroscience (2015) *Parts of the Nervous System* [Online]. Available from: http://www.brainfacts.org/brain-basics/neuroanatomy/articles/2012/parts-of-the-nervous-system/ [Accessed 05 July 2015].

Tobin, J. (2004) The Disappearance of the Body in Early Childhood Education. In Bresler, L. (ed.) *Knowing Bodies, Moving Minds: Towards Embodied teaching and Learning*, pp.111–125. Dordrecht: Kluwer Academic Publishers.

Tortora, G.J., & Anagnostakos, N.P. (1990) Principles of Anatomy and Physiology (6th edn.), pp.336–337. New York: Harper (cited in Hannaford 2005:44).

Tovey, H. (2014) EYFS Best Practice: All About … Risk [Online]. Available from http://www.nurseryworld.co.uk/digital_assets/291/LDAllaboutRisk.pdf [Accessed 26 November 2015].

Towne Jennings, J. (2008) *Touting Tummy Time* [Online]. Available from: http://physical-therapy.advanceweb.com/Article/Touting-Tummy-Time.aspx [Accessed 14 August 2015].

Vygotsky,L. (1978) *Mind in Society: Development of Higher Psychological Processes.* Cambridge, MA: Harvard University Press.

Walsh, D.J. (2004) Frog Boy and the American Monkey. In Bresler, L. (ed.) *Knowing Bodies, Moving Minds: Towards Embodied Teaching and Learning*, pp.97–109. Dordrecht: Kluwer Academic Publishers.

Whitebread, D., & Sinclair-Harding, L. (2014) EYFS Best Practice: All About … Neuroscience and the Infant Brain *Nursery World* [Online]. Available from: www.nurseryworld.co.uk [Accessed 10 September 2015].

Wilke, S., Opdenakker, C.,Kremers, S.P.J., & Gubbels, J. (2014) *Factors Influencing Childcare Workers' Promotion of Physical Activity in Children aged 0–4: A Qualitative Study* [Online]. Available from: http://www.ncbi.nlm.nih.gov/pmc/articles/PMC4002539/ [Accessed 28 August].

Winter, P. (2010) *Engaging Families in the Early Childhood Development Story* [Online]. Australian Educational Services Ltd. Available from: http://www.scseec.edu.au/site/DefaultSite/filesystem/documents/Reports%20and%20publications/Publications/Early%20childhood%20education/Engaging%20Families%20in%20the%20ECD%20Story-Neuroscience%20and%20ECD.pdf [Accessed 23 November 2015].

Wolff, P. (1968) Sucking Patterns of Infant Mammals. *Brain, Behaviour and Evolution* 1, 354–367 (cited in Goddard Blythe 2009).

Index

Note: 'F' after a page number indicates a figure.